Administering College and University Housing: A Legal Perspective

Edited by

DONALD D. GEHRING

COLLEGE ADMINISTRATION PUBLICATIONS, INC.

College Administration Publications, Inc.,
P. O. Box 8492, Asheville, N. C. 28814

© 1983 College Administration Publications, Inc.,
All rights reserved. Published 1983
Printed in the United States of America

Library of Congress Cataloging in Publication Data

Main entry under title:

Administering college and university housing.

    Bibliography: p.
    1. Student housing—Law and legislation—United
States. I. Gehring, Donald D.
KF4243.A93   1983   344.73'0794   83-7257
ISBN 0-912557-00-1   347.304794

The views expressed in this book are those of the individual authors and are not necessarily those of College Administration Publications, Inc.

This publication is designed to provide accurate and
authoritative information in regard to the subject
matter covered. It is sold with the understanding that
the publisher is not engaged in rendering legal, ac-
counting or other professional service. If legal advice
or other expert assistance is required, the services of
a competent professional person should be sought.

*—from a Declaration of Principles jointly adopted by a
committee of the American Bar Association and a committee of publishers.*

Table of Contents

Preface

In recent years almost every aspect of college and university administration has been subject to judicial scrutiny. Campus housing has not been immune to such litigation. The very nature and diversity of campus housing demands that everyone on the housing staff be familiar with the legal issues involved in the daily administration of the program.

This monograph is intended to provide a basic introduction to the legal issues involved in the operation and administration of college and university housing programs. Being sensitive to these issues can not only reduce the risk of liability but can also result in more equitable policies and practices. The monograph is written for the practicing housing administrator, but it could also serve as a valuable aid in professional preparation programs.

Generally, the law is no different for housing than it is for any other campus administrative area. The information presented in this monograph applies to every aspect of institutional administration. What makes the monograph unique, however, is that it is written from a campus housing perspective in order to make it more meaningful to housing administrators. This perspective is achieved by illustrating concepts using housing case law wherever possible. Thus, the housing administrator will not only be able to relate to the discussion better, but will learn some housing case law at the same time. In addition, each of the authors has campus housing experience which they bring to bear in presenting their material.

The chapters are written in layman's language and legal terminology has been avoided wherever possible. The reader will not need a legal background to find the monograph informative and useful. The publication is intended for everyone on the housing staff—from the Director to the R.A. The authors have compiled a Checklist of

Housing Legal Issues which can be used as an audit of housing policies or as a tool for staff development.

For those who wish to approach a topic in more depth, a Table of Cases has been provided which lists the complete citation for each case referenced in the text. References to materials other than cases, are listed at the end of each chapter. Appendices listing the geographic area covered by each United States Court of Appeals and abbreviations for publications in the National Reporter System have been provided to assist in finding cited cases. Another appendix provides references to federal laws and regulations affecting campus housing.

Each chapter addresses a series of separate issues. The reader may find the information most beneficial if read in sequence; however, sequential reading is not necessary. Those well versed in a particular area may wish to skip that chapter altogether or only read a portion of it for clarification on a particular point.

The chapters progress logically beginning with a basic introduction setting forth a rationale for staff training in legal issues and the relationships which define the rights and responsibilities of students, staff, and the institution. These relationships also provide the framework for the remaining chapters. Chapter II addresses the most common constitutional issues faced in administering housing programs. The chapter also contains unique sections on group sanctions and "psychiatric withdrawals." Specific federal laws affecting student policies and staff employment practices are discussed in Chapter III. Key words to assist administrators in finding state laws have also been included in this chapter. One of the most prevalent relationships which exists in campus housing is explored in Chapter IV where the focus is the contract. The elements of a contract are set forth in general terms and then applied specifically to the housing situation. Administrative liability for negligence is the topic in Chapter V. The elements of the tort of negligence and defenses which can possibly shield the administrator, provide the keystone for this chapter. The final chapter brings into perspective the potential liability facing housing administrators by examining ways to manage the risks.

Throughout the monograph, the authors caution that there is no substitute for legal counsel. The information contained in this publication is intended to assist housing staff recognize the legal issues involved in their daily activity. Recognition of these issues is a necessary first step, but only a first step. Obtaining competent legal counsel is the second step. Hopefully, this monograph will assist you in learning to take both those steps.

Donald D. Gehring, *Editor*
Louisville, Kentucky
December 15, 1982

About the Authors

The first four authors listed have served on the faculty of the ACUHO–I College, Legal Issues Institute.

DONALD D. GEHRING, Ed.D., is currently Associate Professor of Higher Education at the University of Louisville and serves as Co-Editor of *The College Student and the Courts*. He edits all state higher education cases for the National Organization for Legal Problems in Education and serves on the ACUHO–I Legislative Issues Committee. Dr. Gehring is a graduate of Georgia Institute of Technology, Emory University and the University of Georgia. He has extensive housing experience, having served as a hall director and Supervisor of Men's Housing at Emory University and Director of Housing at West Georgia College. He has published extensively in the area of college and university legal issues.

TOM MILLER, J.D., is Director of Housing at Princeton University where he has full responsibility for undergraduate, graduate, faculty/staff and guest housing. He has previously served as Assistant Dean of Men and Associate Director of Residential Living at the University of Pennsylvania. Tom holds the Bachelors degree in Industrial Management from Carnegie Tech and earned his law degree at the University of Pennsylvania. For the past nine years he has taught law at the Wharton School of the University of Pennsylvania. He has also taught and coached debate and public speaking at St. Joseph's College, Rosemont College and the University of Pennsylvania.

DONALD R. MOORE, J.D., is a past president of ACUHO–I. Currently he serves as Vice President and Dean for Student Services at Tulane University. He has twenty-seven years of experience in different administrative positions in higher education which includes service as Director of Housing at Emory University and Tulane University. Don earned his Bachelors degree and his law degree at Emory University. He is also a past president of both SEAHO and SWACHO.

GARY PAVELA, J.D., is Director of Judicial Programs at the University of Maryland–College Park, where he also teaches courses in constitutional and administrative law. He has been a law clerk to the Chief Judge of the United States Court of Appeals for the Tenth Circuit, a Fellow at the University of Wisconsin Center for Behavioral Science and Law, and a consultant to the Federal Judicial Center in Washington, D.C. He is a Phi Beta Kappa graduate of Lawrence College in Wisconsin, holds advanced degrees in history and in education from Wesleyan University in Connecticut, and a law degree from the University of Illinois. While at Illinois he served as a head resident in the university residence halls. He is a member of the New York and federal bars.

LARRY MURRAY, B.S., is Assistant to the Vice President for Student Services at Tulane University. He earned his Bachelors degree in Management at Tulane and is currently a senior in the University's School of Law where he is a member of the National Trial Team. Larry has also served as a Resident Advisor and a Senior Advisor in the Housing Department of Tulane.

Chapter I

Legal Information:
A Part of the
Decision Making Process

Donald D. Gehring

As a housing administrator, whether an R.A. or a Director, you are frequently called upon to make decisions. These decisions may range from how to approach a roommate conflict to deciding where to locate the next set of apartments. Effective decision making requires information and the evaluation of alternatives.

Basic information about the legal framework within which daily decisions are made, is extremely important if you are to operate a sound housing program. Decisions which affect the rights of students and employees, or obligate the institution, simply cannot be made without considering legal consequences and parameters. Does this mean that you need to be an attorney? Certainly not. Attorneys are trained legal specialists and there is no substitute for legal counsel when you need to know the law affecting a particular situation. However, everyone on the housing staff needs to be sensitive to the *legal issues* which may arise in the daily management of the housing operation.

Being able to recognize the legal issues involved in a particular situation can serve as a warning for you. When staff are alert to these warnings, they know to proceed with regard for the rights and responsibilities involved in the situation. A familiarity with the basic relationships which exist between students, staff, and the institution and the rights and obligations that these relationships create, is essential if you are to recognize the red-flag warnings.

WHY STUDY LEGAL ISSUES?

There are several reasons for developing a sensitivity to the legal issues involved in campus housing. Reducing the amount of anxiety within the staff, is a management activity which can pay dividends. Staff members who are familiar with the legal relationships which exist between themselves, students, and the institution, are more likely

1

to use that information in their day-to-day decisions. They are also more likely to recognize problem areas and seek assistance. Over time, they are thus more likely to exhibit confidence in their decision making ability, and therefore, satisfaction with the employment environment.

College and university housing is a full partner in the student development movement. Living-learning centers often led the way on campus as an initial effort to facilitate the total development of students. Campus housing is still in the forefront of student development efforts on many campuses.

Assisting students to understand their rights and responsibilities as citizens is certainly an important aspect of their personal development. One of the principles of student development theory states that the entire environment is educational and should be used to facilitate development. Staff who recognize the legal issues involved in various situations, are in a better position to use those situations as learning experiences to enhance the moral and ethical development of students.

Another obvious reason for developing an understanding of the legal issues involved in the administration of college housing is to avoid expensive and time-consuming litigation. The consumer movement in higher education and the general litigious nature of our society makes you, as the housing administrator, particularly vulnerable to suit.

Many aspects of college and university housing involve specific services paid for by students. In addition, campus housing is where residential students spend most of their time. Both the nature of the service provided and the frequency of contact demand that as a housing administrator, you need to be aware of the legal issues in managing this complex area. Even where litigation does not involve a suit for damages against the individual administration, the time, money, effort and sheer psychological energy expended in defending a particular decision can be very costly.

Developing a sensitivity to the legal issues involved in the daily administration of campus housing is an important skill for RA's and Hall Directors to gain. These individuals are "on the firing line" and often called upon to make immediate decisions without the benefit of consultation with higher authority. The RA who recognizes that a particular situation may involve a denial of an individual's rights, or other legal issues, may choose to postpone making a decision if possible. If, on the other hand, the RA was faced with a similar situation in the past and obtained consultation, there is already a basis for making a decision. Training for housing staff in the area of legal issues should be part of every staff development program. Since the RA will often be found to be acting as an "agent" of the institution, the Director, or other superiors could be held liable for the actions of the RA under the legal theory of "respondeat superior."

RELATIONSHIPS WITH STUDENTS AND STAFF

In order to recognize legal issues arising in the daily operation of housing, you need to understand the basic relationships which exist between the institution, students and staff. These relationships define the rights of the college or university and the individual involved. Thus, the decision making process must include a determination of the relationship involved which will, in turn, reveal the rights affected.

There are five basic relationships which exist between campus housing, as an organizational unit of the institution, and students and staff. Students and staff are citizens and as such, they have a constitutional relationship with the housing departments at public institutions. In both public and private institutions, students and staff also have a contractual relationship with the housing office. The contractual relationship may either be explicit or implied. Both types of institutions must, in addition to contractual rights, also respect the person, property and reputation of students and staff. Failure to do so could result in a tort, or twisted relationship, for which the institution or individual staff member could be held liable. Applicable federal or state laws may also define a relationship between the parties. Finally, administrative regulations may create yet another relationship and set of rights.

The relationships outlined above, are defined or created in state and federal constitutions, statutes and regulations, contracts and case law. The last source, case law, consists of judicial opinions interpreting the other documents and providing remedies not found in the statutes. Case law is sometimes referred to as *judge-made* law.

SOURCES OF LAW: HOW TO FIND THEM

Your decision making ability as a housing administrator could be greatly enhanced by having access to the sources of law which define the relationships between housing and others. One need not be an attorney to be able to find and read the law. While there are some terms which have specific legal meanings, the administrator can gain a good general understanding of rights and obligations by reading the constitutional provisions, statutes, regulations and cases pertaining to college housing. There simply is no substitute for reading the original source.

Constitutions

Federal and state constitutions can usually be found in the reference room of most college libraries. The United States Constitution is the supreme law of the land and everything else must be in accord with the Constitution. While federal and state constitutions are very broad documents, they do outline the rights and limitations of government, as well as the rights of citizens. Housing officers should be particularly interested in the First, Fourth and Fourteenth Amendments of the federal Constitution. Annotated copies of these documents are often available. The annotations explain the history of a particular section and how it has been interpreted.

Statutes

The laws passed by Congress, such as Title IX or Section 504, are codified in the *United States Code (U.S.C.)*. The *United States Code Annotated (U.S.C.A.)* and the *United States Code Service (U.S.C.S.)* are two commercial publications which also contain the codified laws of the United States with annotations. One or more of these publications often will be found in the library reference room. Individual law offices or the county court building will have copies of these publications too. The Code is organized by topics and includes many volumes. Title 20 of the Code contains the laws specifically related to education, while Title 42 refers to public health and welfare laws. Each publication has its own index.

The Arabic numbers should not be confused with Roman numerals. Roman numerals, such as Title IX, refer to a specific part of a law passed by Congress. In the case of Title IX, the number refers to a specific part of the Education Amendments of 1972. Once the Higher Education Amendments of 1972 became a federal law, Title IX (along with other titles in the Act) was codified as a "section" within Title 20 of the Code. References to the Code (or *citations* as they are generally referred to) will be written with the title number first, the name of the publication next and the specific section last. Thus, for example, 20 *U.S.C.S.*, 401 would refer to Title 20 (educational laws) in the *United States Code Service* section 401 (The National Defense Education Act). The symbol "§" is often used and simply means "section."

State laws are also codified in several volumes for each state. Topics (such as colleges and universities) in the state codes are usually organized by chapter and contain annotations giving interpretations of the statute. Citations to state laws also use Arabic numerals. The name of the state laws usually appears first, followed by a reference to the chapter and section. Chapters and sections are normally separated by a period or hyphen. For example, KRS 164.891 refers to Kentucky Revised Statutes (KRS), Chapter 164 (Colleges and Universities), Section 891 (defining "agents," for purposes of malpractice insurance, at the University of Louisville).

You will find one or more index volumes at the end of the statutes. To find topics of interest, simply look under key words, as in any other index. For example, to determine if there are any state laws on hazing, one would look under *colleges and universities, hazing, students, fraternities and sororities*, or similar topics. State statutes

4

can normally be found in the reference room of the library, individual law offices or the county court building. Public libraries will usually also have copies of the state statutes. To gain a basic familiarity with your state laws, you would benefit greatly from simply perusing the index for topics of interest, finding and reading them.

Because the law is ever changing, both the federal code and state statutes have updates filed in the back of the volumes. These "pocket parts," as they are called, are organized and numbered in the same way as the code or statutes, and are simply a way to update the hardback volume without replacing it everytime a new law is passed. Whenever one reads a law in the hardback volume, the "pocket part" should also be checked to ensure that the law has not subsequently been repealed, or changed in some way.

Regulations

A statute or law passed by the Congress or a state legislature, is very broad in scope. Thus, the legislative body will require administrative agencies to develop rules and regulations to implement the law. Regulations of federal agencies first appear in the *Federal Register* (*F.R.*). Once those regulations have been approved and published in their final form, they are codified and incorporated into the *Code of Federal Regulations* (*C.F.R.*). The *F.R.* and the *C.F.R.* can generally be found in the federal documents section of the college library or the reference room. United States Attorneys and federal court houses will also maintain copies. State administrative regulations can usually be found at any state agency, such as at public colleges and universities.

The citation system for federal and most state administrative regulations parallels that used for the *U.S. Code*. Thus, 34 *C.F.R.* 84 would refer to Title 34 (education topic) of the *Code of Federal Regulations*, part 84 (regulations dealing with nondiscrimination on the basis of handicap, in educational institutions). In Kentucky, 11 KAR 5:030 refers to Title 11 (Kentucky Higher Education Assistance Authority) of the Kentucky Administrative Regulations (KAR) Chapter 5 (KHEAA grant programs) section 030 (student eligibility).

Case Law

Not everyone agrees on the specific interpretation of a particular constitutional provision, statute, regulation or contractual provision. When such controversies arise, the courts are asked to render a decision. These judicial opinions are referred to as case law and provide yet another source of law. Courts sometimes even fashion a remedy where none presently exists.

Judicial decisions are published in a series of reporters. Federal cases can be decided at three different levels, thus there is at least one publication reporting decisions at each level. The United States Supreme Court is the highest court in the land and its opinions are so significant that they appear in several publications. The federal government publishes Supreme Court decisions in the *United States Reports (U.S.)*. *The Supreme Court Reporter (S.Ct.)*; *Lawyers Edition* 2d *(L.Ed.2d)*; and the *United States Law Week (L.W.)* are commercial publications which report the Supreme Court's decisions.

Current decisions of United States Courts of Appeals are reported in the second series of the *Federal Reporter (F.2d)*. These courts have jurisdiction over specific geographic areas (see Appendix A). Federal district courts also exercise jurisdiction within a particular area and their decisions are reported in the *Federal Supplement (F. Supp.)*. Some district court decisions may also be found in the *Federal Rules Digest (F.R.D.)*.

Each state has a similar hierarchical system of courts. Normally, only the decisions of state appellate courts are reported. State court decisions are published in a reporter system covering several states (see Appendix B). For example, the current decisions of the appellate courts of Maine, New Hampshire, Vermont, Connecticut, New Jersey, Pennsylvania, Delaware and Maryland would appear in the second series of the *Atlantic Reporter (A.2d)*.

All published decisions are cited in a similar fashion. The first name in the citation generally refers to the person bringing the complaint—the plaintiff, or appellee. The second name refers to the individual defending against the action—the defendant, or appellant. There will then be several arabic numerals, followed by an abbreviation and then more numerals. The abbreviation indicates the reporter in which the decision is published; the first set of numerals indicates the volume of that publication, in which it appears; and the second set refers to the page number on which the case may be found in the volume. Finally, there will be a set of parentheses. Information in the parentheses indicates the specific court which rendered the decision and the year the case was decided. Since there is only one United States Supreme Court, only the year appears in the parentheses for citations to it's opinions. Citations to state supreme court opinions will only show the abbreviation for the particular state, and the year, in parentheses.

Thus, *Widmar* v. *Vincent*, 102 *S. Ct.* 269 (1981) is a decision of the United States Supreme Court appearing in volume 102 of the *Supreme Court Reporter* on page 269. The case was decided in 1981 and involved a controversy between Widmar and Vincent. *Emory University* v. *Porubiansky*, 282 *S.E.2d* 903 (Ga., 1981) was a controversy between Emory University and Porubiansky decided by the Georgia Supreme Court in 1981. The court's decision may be found on page 903 of volume 282 of the *Southeastern Reporter*, Second Series.

Federal and state reporters can be located in attorney's offices, state or federal court buildings, and law school libraries. Local bar associations often maintain a law library containing both federal and state reporters. Local individual attorneys are more likely to maintain state reporters, while U.S. Attorneys will usually maintain the federal reporter system.

THE JURISDICTION OF COURTS

The three federal courts which you are most concerned with are federal district courts, United States courts of appeals and The Supreme Court. There are many district courts, but only twelve courts of appeals and only one Supreme Court. These courts are all courts of geographic jurisdiction. What that means is simply that they only have jurisdiction over matters which arise in a specific geographic area. This also means that the decision of a court in one geographic jurisdiction generally does not bind another jurisdiction. Thus, when the District Court for the Western District of Michigan decides an issue, the District Court for the Southern District of New York might decide a similar issue differently. Of course, the New York District Court could adopt the reasoning of the Michigan Court and decide the issue similarly if it choses to do so.

The courts of appeals are also courts of geographic jurisdiction. Prior to 1982, several courts of appeals had decided that it was the intent of Title IX to include employees under the scope of the Act. At the same time, several other courts of appeals held that Title IX was only intended to prohibit sex discrimination against students, and employees were not within the scope of Title IX. This difference was possible because the courts only have jurisdiction over their own specific geographic area (see Appendix A).

Obviously, the country can't operate with federal law being interpreted differently in different parts of the land. That's where the Supreme Court comes in. The Supreme Court has jurisdiction over the entire nation and its possessions. When the Supreme Court speaks, everyone listens! With respect to Title IX, the Supreme Court has recently held, in *North Haven Board of Education* v. *Bell* (1982), that employees are covered within the scope of the Act.

State courts are generally organized along the lines of the federal system—hierarchical and with geographic jurisdiction. This type of system has promoted the statement that "The law is what the highest court says it is!" States, like the federal system, also have courts of "special," rather than geographic, jurisdiction. You will be especially interested in the Court of Claims, which is where many states require claims against state agencies to be settled.

You should also be aware that the laws of each state differ and judicial interpretations in one state have no binding effect on another state. What Indiana courts decide, with regard to the liability of a social host for the torts of an intoxicated guest, has no bind-

7

ing effect on what the Kentucky courts might decide for the same issue. A well reasoned opinion, however, might carry a good deal of sway for other jurisdictions.

WORKING WITH INSTITUTIONAL COUNSEL

Increasingly, universities and colleges are appointing "in-house" attorneys. Certainly, having counsel right on campus is convenient and comforting. However, whether one has "in-house" counsel, or uses a local attorney on a retainer basis, there are several aspects related to working with counsel that you need to be aware of and address.

No matter what kind of legal counsel an institution has, you need to determine how to obtain access to those services. Institutions will generally have set procedures for consulting with the attorney or, in some cases, the firm that represents the university. The administrator should learn what those procedures are *before* there is a need to use them. Almost invariably, a critical question will arise after normal working hours. How does one gain access to counsel in such emergencies? Could counsel be reached at home if needed? Who should initiate contact with counsel . . . during working hours . . . after working hours . . . on weekends?.

Once access to counsel has been established, how should the attorney be used to benefit you as a housing administrator? There are several ways in which the institution's attorney can be helpful to college housing administrators. Counsel may, with the assistance of housing staff, conduct professional development seminars or workshops. It's important, however, that you and the housing staff work with the attorney in planning and preparing for such programs. While counsel knows the law and is the one person to provide legal advice, the housing staff is most familiar with the reality of residence hall operations. Both areas of knowledge have to be blended if the program is to be helpful to staff.

Counsel can also be very effective in responding to specific concerns of staff. These concerns should usually be put to counsel in the form of a question. Since there are very few absolutes in the law, questions should not be phrased in such a way as to evoke a *yes* or *no* response. Although it's tempting to want a yes or no response, it's very difficult for counsel to respond in such a way without knowing the complete set of facts. For example, asking whether an RA can copy material from a copyrighted publication to use in an alcohol abuse workshop would be difficult to answer. A better question might be "under what conditions may R.A.'s copy material from a protected work, to use in an educational workshop?" This latter question would provide information that can be used in the decision making process. Knowing what questions to ask is yet another reason for becoming familiar with the legal issues inherent in housing operations.

8

Another way in which counsel can be of benefit to you as a housing administrator is to respond to draft copies of policies, forms, handbooks, contracts, licenses and similar materials. Counsel should be asked to review such material *before* it is finalized. Responses of counsel to these documents can point out problems, different interpretations, unintended obligations or promises and the like. Responses from counsel should be provided in writing, for reference purposes, and to document your good faith effort in acting on advice of counsel.

Housing documents and materials should be reviewed by counsel not only whenever there is a change but also every few years, even where there have not been any changes. The law is very dynamic and a policy that was legally acceptable a few years ago may be an infringement on someone's rights today.

Using counsel in these ways can be beneficial to you as a housing administrator, but only if you, and counsel, both recognize your responsibilities and limitations in the process. Housing administrators are not attorneys and should therefore rely on counsel to draw the legal guidelines and parameters. However, attorneys are not housing administrators and should not attempt to make administrative decisions.

The housing officer who allows counsel to make administrative decisions abdicates responsibility for the housing program. There is usually a risk associated with every decision. As a housing officer, you are in the best position to know if the educational advantages of a particular decision outweigh the risk of potential liability. What counsel can do is help you and your staff to understand what can be done to minimize the risk, once an educational decision has been made within the legal parameters.

SUMMARY

A study of this monograph can prepare you to get the most out of working with counsel by sensitizing you to the legal issues which affect your work. As part of a professional library, you should have a good basic text in college law in addition to this monograph. Such a publication will provide a more detailed presentation of aspects, other than housing, and provide you with an overall view of the legal issues in the institution as a whole. In addition, you or your office should subscribe to an updating service to keep abreast of the ever changing case law as it relates to college housing. By staying current and assisting others with whom you work to do the same, you will reduce the risk of infringing upon someone elses rights.

Chapter II

Constitutional Issues In the Residence Halls

Gary Pavela

INTRODUCTION

The basic guarantees of individual liberties found in the Constitution were not always applied on campus. Students could be dismissed because they failed to attend religious services at a state university (*North*, 1891); because they were "apparently not in sympathy with the management of the institution" (*Woods*, 1924, p. 550); or simply because they publicly criticized the campus administration (*Steier*, 1959). Although nearly everyone understands that these cases do not reflect the current state of the law, many educators fail to ask how college and university students managed to acquire a number of important substantive and procedural rights over the years, especially at public schools. An appropriate answer would be that while the Constitution has changed relatively little since the turn of the century, the social and political perspective of the judiciary has changed a great deal.

When judges interpret the Constitution, they occasionally attempt to convey the impression that they are implementing the intentions of the Founding Fathers. Actually, as Richard Neely (1981) has observed, "[W]hat the courts are really saying . . . is that if the Founding Fathers had grown up in the twentieth century, had had all of our experiences, and perceived the problems from our vantage point, they would decide the case the way the court writing the opinion is deciding it"(p. 11). This means, of course, that constitutional law is not static; it develops and evolves as social change occurs in the larger society.

The effect of social change upon constitutional interpretation is demonstrated by a lawsuit which ultimately revolutionized many aspects of college and university law. In *Dixon*, (1961), the United States Court of Appeals for the Fifth Circuit heard a case involving the expulsion of a number of Black students from Alabama State College. The students, who were dismissed without a hearing, had participated in civil rights demonstrations off campus, which the president of the college regarded as being disruptive "to the orderly conduct of [college] business" (p. 152). Disregarding all precedent to the contrary, the Court of Appeals reinstated the students and held that a charge of misconduct depends upon a determination of facts "easily colored by the point of view of the witnesses," thereby requiring "the rudiments of an adversary proceeding" in which college authorities would have "an opportunity to hear both sides in considerable detail" (p. 159).

The holding in *Dixon* is significant not only for what it tells us about the Constitution, but also because it demonstrates that educators who violate the evolving standards of basic fairness in our society are likely to run afoul of the law. The president of Alabama State College in 1961 simply lived in a different social environment than his predecessors. By misunderstanding the impact of the civil rights movement upon his college (and upon the country as a whole), he became an unwilling participant in a process which changed the way the Constitution would be applied on campus.

Unfortunately, too many educators who are familiar with cases such as *Dixon* assume that they can affect the development of constitutional law only by doing something wrong. In many instances, however, it is also possible to influence the law by doing something right. For example, in *Bakke* (1978), the Supreme Court held that a special admissions program used by the University of California at Davis was unconstitutional. At the same time, Justice Powell cited the "illuminating example" of a Harvard College admissions program, which encouraged minority enrollment without setting a specific racial quota. Likewise, in *Board of Curators* v. *Horowitz* (1978), the Supreme Court determined that a student at a public institution of higher education need not be accorded a hearing prior to being dismissed for academic deficiencies. An important factor taken into consideration by the Court was an innovative due process procedure developed by the University (i.e., evaluation of the student's academic performance by an independent panel of practitioners), which convinced even a dissenting Justice that the student in question had been accorded "as much procedural protection as the Due Process Clause requires" (p. 103, Justice Marshall, concurring in part and dissenting in part).

The list of useful contributions which school officials have made to the evolution of constitutional law could be cited at length. Nonetheless, the principle remains the same: the various words and phrases in the Constitution are defined by judges who are influenced by events in the larger society. As an institutional administrator who understands this process, you can anticipate (and affect) the ways in which the Constitution will be applied on your campus by carefully monitoring the basic "fairness" of your policies, both from your own perspective, and from the perspective of responsible individuals in the larger community. The discussion which follows is designed to be of assistance to you in this regard by defining current trends in the law on matters related to "state action" and private schools, freedom of expression, search and seizure, and the application of the Fourteenth Amendment at institutions of higher education.

THE CONSTITUTION AND PRIVATE INSTITUTIONS

The various protections in the Bill of Rights were originally enacted as limitations solely upon the federal government (*Barron*, 1833). It was not until long after the Fourteenth Amendment was adopted that most of those protections were also applied to the actions of states and localities. So far, most courts have not extended the same constitutional restrictions to private schools (Kaplin, 1978; Thigpen, 1982; *Rendell-Baker*, 1982; *Green*, 1979; *Grossner*, 1968).

Private school administrators should not conclude that they are unaffected by developments in constitutional law. There have been cases in which private schools have been held to be so intertwined with the state that they must comply with the provisions of the Fourteenth Amendment (*Ryan*, 1971; *Isaacs*, 1974). Furthermore, private schools are subject to federal statutes and regulations which may follow constitutional standards. The federal handicap regulations, for example, contain especially broad language requiring most recipient institutions to adopt grievance systems with "appropriate due process" procedures (45 *C.F.R.* 84.7 [b]).

Private schools may also have contractual obligations to students which resemble constitutional due process requirements (*Clayton*, 1981). These obligations need not be specified in a formal document. For example, in *Carr* (1962), it was held that:

> there is an implied contract between the student and the university that, if he complies with the terms prescribed by the university, he will obtain the degree which he sought. The university cannot take the student's money . . . and then arbitrarily expel him or arbitrarily refuse, when he has completed the required courses, to confer on him that which it promised, namely, the degree. (p. 413)

Finally, private school officials may wish to adhere to fundamental constitutional norms as a matter of policy. Contrary to popular impression, the courts have not saddled public campuses with burdensome due process requirements (see the discussion of Fourteenth Amendment due process standards in this chapter). There does not appear to be any sound reason for private schools to reject the simple standards of basic fairness which are applicable at state supported institutions.

THE FIRST AMENDMENT

The First Amendment to the Constitution states that:

Congress shall make no law respecting an establishment of religion, or prohibiting the free exercise thereof; or abridging the freedom of speech, or of the press, or the right of the people peaceably to assemble, and to petition the Government for a redress of grievances.

Although the plain wording of the First Amendment would restrict only the power of "Congress," the Supreme Court held in 1939 that it should be applied to the states as well (*Schneider*, 1939). Furthermore, a number of state constitutions have comparable provisions which may be applicable to both public and private institutions (*State*, 1982).

The Supreme Court has held that there is "no room for the view that, because of the acknowledged need for order, First Amendment protections should apply with less force on college campuses than in the community at large" (*Healy*, 1972, p. 180). An underlying rationale for this commitment was stated in *Keyishian* (1967):

Our Nation is deeply committed to safeguarding academic freedom which is of transcendent value to all of us . . . .. The nation's future depends upon leaders trained through wide exposure to that robust exchange of ideas which discovers truth out of a multitude of tongues, rather than through any kind of authoritative selection. (p. 603, citation omitted)

The various protections specified in the First Amendment are stated as absolutes. Nonetheless, public officials have been permitted over the years to prohibit the dissemination of certain types of expression (e.g., obscenity) and to impose reasonable restrictions upon the time, place, and manner in which First Amendment rights are exercised. These limitations upon the scope of the First Amendment can be best understood by considering a number of pertinent problems which may arise on the campus, and particularly in your residence halls.

Freedom of Speech

One problem occasionally encountered by housing officials is the use of offensive language in the halls. It can be a great temptation to assert that this form of expression has no place in the campus environment and to punish those responsible for it. The Supreme Court has determined, however, that "the mere dissemination of ideas—no matter how offensive to good taste—on a state university campus, may not be shut off in the name alone of 'conventions of decency'" (*Papish*, 1973, p. 670). Even the expression of a four letter vulgarity addressed to a public university president can be protected by the Constitution (*Thoren*, 1973).

The courts do, however, see a difference between vulgarity and obscenity. The latter, as defined in *Miller* (1973), is not considered a form of speech protected by the First Amendment. Under the *Miller* standard, material may be considered obscene if it:

1. depicts or describes, in a "patently offensive way," sexual conduct specifically defined by applicable state law; and
2. taken as a whole, appeals to "prurient interest in sex;" and
3. taken as a whole, does "not have serious literary, artistic, political, or scientific value" (p. 24).

The law pertaining to obscenity can be very complex. Distinctions need to be made, for example, between the private possession of obscene material and its distribution (*Stanley*, 1969). Likewise, officials at public institutions should understand that any system of prior restraint or censorship will bear "a heavy presumption against its constitutional validity" (*Southeastern Promotions Ltd*, 1975, p. 558). It will be imperative to consult with counsel before developing and enforcing any obscenity standard on campus.

As a housing administrator, you may also seek to regulate various forms of expression which could be defamatory. Defamation consists of words which are written (libel) or spoken (slander) which communicate false information, damaging to a person's reputation. For example, you would properly be concerned about the publication of a residence hall newspaper which appeared to contain libelous material. As in the case of obscenity, however, the regulation or prohibition of free expression on the grounds of potential libel, should be undertaken with extreme care, if at all. The courts will require school administrators to conduct a careful inquiry into whether the material is libelous as a matter of state law (*Trujillo*, 1971). Furthermore, broadly written policies designed to prevent the publication of libelous material may be viewed as an effort to suppress legitimate dissent on campus (*Baughman*, 1973). In short, it might be best for you to use the publication as a learning opportunity and advise students about the legal issues pertaining to libel, rather than relying upon any form of censorship. If necessary, the housing office may publicly disassociate itself from a student publication (*Bazaar*, 1973). In any event, by recognizing student rights and responsibilities in this regard, you can limit the potential liability of the institution and your staff for the publication of defamatory material (*Mazart*, 1981; see, generally, Stevens, 1975).

Another form of speech which is currently testing the limits of the Constitution on campus is the expression of racist remarks and epithets. Administrators are not powerless to respond to such behavior if the manner of expression is disruptive (e.g., classes are interrupted by a loudspeaker), or if it is accompanied by damage to property (e.g., painting a symbol on a school building), or by specific threats of violence (*Norton*, 1969). The courts have held, however, that the simple assertion of racist sentiments can be protected by the First Amendment (Joyner, 1973).

One rationale for protecting offensive and insulting forms of speech was set forth by Justice Hugo Black, who observed that "First Amendment [freedoms] must be accorded to ideas we hate, or sooner or later they will be denied to the ideas we cherish" (*Communist Party*, 1961, p. 137). The Supreme Court has cited this principle in holding that even an organization such as the Ku Klux Klan has a right to freedom of expression (*Brandenburg*, 1969). Perhaps the clearest statement of the applicable First Amendment standard was made by the United States Court of Appeals for the Fourth Circuit in *National Socialist White Peoples' Party* (1973):

> [T]he expression of racist and anti-Semitic views in a public place and the right to assemble in a public place for the purpose of communicating and discussing racist and anti-Semitic views are protected activities and may not be circumscribed by the state, except where advocacy is directed to inciting or producing imminent lawless action and is likely to incite or produce such action. (p. 1015, citation omitted)

It should be emphasized that administrators at private institutions have more latitude than their counterparts at public colleges and universities to prohibit any expression of racist views on campus. Before embarking on that course, however, careful consideration will need to be given to the scope and wording of any prohibition and to the need to protect academic freedom. For instance, broadly worded prohibitions against "racist" speech on campus might logically apply to literary works such as *The Merchant of Venice* and could lead to official censorship of library materials. A Yale University committee considered these issues in 1975, and endorsed a policy quite similar to what would be required at public institutions:

> Shock, hurt and anger are not consequences to be weighed lightly. No member of the community with a decent respect for others should use, or encourage others to use, slurs and epithets intended to discredit another's race, ethnic group, religion, or sex . . . [But] even when some members of the university community fail to meet their social and ethical responsibilities, the paramount obligation of the university is to protect their right to free expression. If the university's overriding commitment to free expression is to be sustained, secondary social and ethical responsibilities must be left to the informal processes of suasion, example and argument. (*Report of the Committee*, p.18)

Time, Place, and Manner Regulations

The protection given to freedom of expression in the United States is truly extraordinary. This does not mean, however, that everyone with opinions to express must be allowed to do so at any time and at any place (*Heffron*, 1981; *Esteban*, 1969; *Barker*, 1968; *Cox*, 1965). You may impose reasonable time, place, and manner restrictions in order to insure that expressive activity does not "drown out classroom

16

conversation, make studying impossible, block entrances" or the like (*Grayned*, 1972, p. 119; see also *Grossner*, 1968; *Goldberg*, 1967).

The regulation of expressive activity by state officials has been subject to very careful scrutiny in the courts. Time, place, and manner restrictions enforced without written standards are especially suspect, as are policies which provide for "blanket discrimination against outsiders" in areas of the campus which might be considered a "public forum" (*Spartacus*, 1980, p. 801). Even in the residence hall setting (which is not normally considered a public forum) it has been held that a total ban against door-to-door political canvassing is impermissible (*James*, 1972).

Valid time, place, and manner restrictions must serve "significant" governmental interests (*Heffron*, 1981). A prohibition against speechmaking in a library reading room, for example, would normally be acceptable, while stringent distribution restrictions applied to a campus newspaper for reasons of "litter control" would not. The latter has been held to be a violation of the "well settled" principle "that minor matters of public inconvenience or annoyance cannot be transformed into substantive evils of sufficient weight to warrant the curtailment of liberty of expression . . ." (*New Times*, 1974, p. 174). Above all else, however, you must avoid imposing restrictions based upon "the content and subject matter of the message communicated" (*Gay Students Organization of the University of New Hampshire*, 1974, p.660).

The most recent example of how the courts will view pertinent time, place, and manner restrictions in the residence hall setting can be found in two cases involving Pennsylvania State University and American Future Systems Inc. (AFS), a company engaged in the sale of tableware and cooking utensils. Penn State allowed AFS to give presentations to groups of students in specified common areas of the residence halls and then to sell merchandise to individual students in their own rooms upon request. What Penn State would not permit was solicitation and selling in common areas, or group presentations or group sales in individual residence hall rooms. AFS contended that this policy constituted an unreasonable infringement of its First Amendment rights.

In *American Future Systems* (1980), the United States Court of Appeals for the Third Circuit concluded that AFS's activity represented a form of "commercial speech" which was entitled to some First Amendment protection. Nonetheless, the court stated that commercial speech holds a "subordinate" position to noncommercial speech and may be subject to more stringent regulation. The residence hall policies in question were held to be reasonable since Penn State made a sufficient showing that "group sales activities within the residence halls would disrupt the proper study atmosphere and the privacy of the students" (p. 257). The court also noted that AFS's freedom of speech had only been "restricted," rather than "totally suppressed."

In a second lawsuit, decided two years later, the same court ruled on another dispute between AFS and Penn State (*American Future Systems*, 1982). This case arose out of Penn State's decision to censor certain portions of the AFS "common area" group presentation in order to prevent any form of "solicitation." While the court reaffirmed the validity of Penn State's distinction between presentation of information and the actual consummation of commercial transaction, it also held that the University "failed to show a substantial state interest, much less a plausible explanation, for its policy differentiating between the nature of the information contained in the AFS demonstration" (p. 913). Furthermore, in remanding the case to a lower court, the Court of Appeals directed that consideration be given to the "associational and free speech rights" of students who might wish to participate in organized presentations in their residence hall rooms.

One cannot read the AFS cases without wondering if the University is motivated by a desire to "protect" students from the questionable tactics of an aggressive sales organization. If so, given the adult status of most students, it might be better to make consumer information available to them rather than resorting to any form of censorship. In any event, a few preliminary conclusions about the AFS litigation are possible. First, college and university residence halls need not be considered a "public forum" for the exercise of First Amendment rights. As a housing administrator, you may restrict those forms of communication which would significantly impinge upon the normal activities which occur in a residential setting. Second, given the limited First Amendment protection accorded to commercial speech, group commercial "transactions" may be banned in the residence halls, at least in residence hall common areas, altogether. Third, college students may have First Amendment "associational" rights to participate in "presentations" or even transactions, in their own rooms. Finally, to the extent that housing officials permit residence hall "common" areas to be used for discussion or debate, the contents of lawful speech occurring there should not be subject to censorship.

Right of Association

One of the unresolved issues in the *American Future Systems* cases was what the court of appeals referred to as the "associational" rights of public college and university students. The Supreme Court has determined in this regard that "the right of individuals to associate, to further their personal beliefs" is "[a]mong the rights protected by the First Amendment" (*Healy*, 1972, p. 181). Predictably, the right of "free association" is the subject of frequent litigation in the college and university setting.

In *Healy*, the Supreme Court considered a case involving denial of recognition by a state college in Connecticut to a local chapter of the Students for a Democratic Society (S.D.S.). Nonrecognition meant that the organization was not permitted to use campus facilities for meetings and other purposes. The Court observed that there "can be no doubt that denial of official recognition, without justification, to college organizations, burdens or abridges [the] associational right," (p. 181), protected by the First Amendment. Denial of recognition would be permitted only if associational activities "infringe reasonable campus rules, interrupt classes, or substantially interfere with the opportunity of the other students to obtain an education" (p. 189). Although the court would permit school officials to "impose a requirement . . . that a group seeking official recognition affirm in advance its willingness to adhere to reasonable campus law" (p. 193), it reiterated that a state school " may not restrict speech or association simply because it finds the views expressed by any group to be abhorrent" (p. 187-188).

The holding in *Healy* has been followed in a number of controversial cases, including cases involving campus-based homosexual organizations (*Department of Education*, 1982; *Gay Lib*, 1977). For example, in *Gay Alliance of Students* (1976), the United States Court of Appeals for the Fourth Circuit held that a public university could not deny "registration" (including use of certain facilities and bulletin boards, listing in a campus directory, and eligibility to obtain university funding) to a gay student group. The University sought to justify the denial of registration on the grounds that the institution would otherwise be perceived as approving the aims and objectives of the Gay Alliance, and because the existence of a registered homosexual group would facilitate unlawful homosexual "contacts." These contentions were rejected by the court, which concluded that registration or recognition of a student group need not be equated with approval of the group's objectives, and that "[i]ndividuals of whatever sexual persuasion have the fundamental right to meet, discuss current problems, and to advocate changes in the *status quo*, so long as there is no 'incitement to imminent lawless action'" (p. 166, citation omitted).

Freedom of Religion
Several recent cases involving campus religious organizations have also affirmed the associational rights of public school students, and the First Amendment right to freedom of religion as well. In *Keegan* (1975), the Supreme Court of Delaware cited the holding in *Healy* to support its conclusion that the University of Delaware could not prohibit religious services in residence hall common areas. The court distinguished between "promotion" and "neutral accommodation" of religion and concluded that:

University policy . . . could be neutral towards religion and could have the primary effect of advancing education by allowing students to meet together in the commons room of their dormitory to exchange ideas and share mutual interests. If any religious group or religion is accommodated or benefited thereby, such accommodation or benefit is purely incidental, and would not, in our judgment, violate the [First Amendment] Establishment Clause . . . .. The commons room is already provided for the benefit of students. It is not a dedication of the space to promote religious interests. (p. 16)

The United States Supreme Court recently reached a similar conclusion and held that a blanket prohibition against use of university facilities for religious purposes was invalid (*Widmar*, 1981). In doing so, the Court reaffirmed its holding in *Healy* and observed that religious worship and discussion in those areas of a public university which might be considered "a generally open forum" are "forms of speech and association protected by the First Amendment" (p. 447). This principle has also been applied by the United States Court of Appeals for the First Circuit in upholding the "associational" rights of a religious group ("CARP") at the University of New Hampshire (*Aman*, 1981).

Summary

1. Students at public colleges and universities are entitled to full First Amendment protection. Students at private schools may have comparable rights based upon state constitutional provisions.
2. The content and subject matter of student expression should not be subject to censorship unless it is determined to be obscene, defamatory, or an incitement to imminent lawless action. Any censorship policy will be subject to very close scrutiny in the courts.
3. Educators may impose reasonable time, place, and manner restrictions to insure that expressive activity does not disrupt the academic environment. Limitations on freedom of expression, however, must be justified by "significant" governmental interests.
4. College and university residence halls need not be considered a "public forum" for the exercise of First Amendment rights. While school officials may not suppress all forms of expressive activity in the residential setting, they may enforce reasonable regulations restricting those forms of communication which would significantly disrupt the normal residence hall environment.
5. A right of "free association" is protected by the First Amendment. Public college and university officials may not restrict or deny recognition to a student group simply because the views expressed by the group are controversial or offensive.
6. Religious worship and discussion conducted in an area which might be considered a "public forum" at a state institution would be protected by the First Amendment.

THE FOURTH AMENDMENT

The Fourth Amendment states that:

> The right of the people to be secure in their persons, houses, papers, and effects, against unreasonable searches and seizures, shall not be violated, and no Warrants shall issue, but upon probable cause, supported by Oath or affirmation, and particularly describing the place to be searched, and the persons or things to be seized.

A fundamental purpose of the Fourth Amendment is to prevent arbitrary governmental invasions of an individual's home or privacy. The amendment reflects the abhorrence which the founders felt for the British "writs of assistance" and is designed to insure that most searches will be authorized by a disinterested magistrate. Furthermore, the amendment has been given a broad interpretation by the courts. It "protects people, not places" and is applicable any time an individual's justifiable expectations of privacy may be infringed by the government (*Katz*, 1967, p. 351). For example, in the educational setting, students normally have justifiable expectations of privacy in their residence hall rooms (*City of Athens*, 1974), their personal possessions (*Johnson*, 1975) and, of course, in their persons (*Horton*, 1982). Furthermore, you cannot require that these privacy rights be waived as a condition of enrollment in the institution or in the residence halls (*Morale*, 1976; *Moore*, 1968).

Officials at private institutions are not normally considered agents of the government and are not bound by the restraints of the Fourth Amendment (*People*, 1974). Consequently, an administrator at a private college who obtained evidence of a crime while conducting a "wrongful search" would not deprive the government of the right to use the evidence in subsequent criminal proceedings (*Walter*, 1980). However, private institutional searches conducted upon the request of the police, or with police participation, would probably require a search warrant (*People*, 1968), as would searches conducted by private security guards for the purpose of criminal prosecution (*People*, 1979). Private college officials should also be alerted to the fact that many states recognize a common law right of privacy which could be used to protect students at both public and private institutions against "unreasonable" intrusions upon their seclusion (3 *Restatement of Torts, Second*, 652 B). For example, the Supreme Court observed in *Rakas* (1978) that one might be able to recover damages for violations of Fourth Amendment rights "or seek redress under state law for invasion of privacy . . .." (p. 134).

Although there is some disagreement, a number of courts have held that officials at tax-supported colleges and universities "are generally deemed to be government agents" in Fourth Amendment cases (*People*, 1974, p. 368; *State*, 1976). Accordingly, it would be useful to understand how the courts define a "search," what exceptions may exist to the requirement that searches be conducted pursuant to a warrant, and what remedies are available to students whose Fourth Amendment rights have been violated. Unfortunately, Fourth Amendment law is very much in flux and is further complicated by the fact that "the Fourth Amendment does not always require the same results in the schools as it does in ordinary circumstances" (*Horton*, 1982, p. 482).

Plain View Exception

It is not considered a "search" for a state official who has a right to be in a certain location to detect something by one of his natural senses. For example, a residence advisor walking down a central hallway does not conduct a "search" when he or she inadvertently overhears a loud conversation occurring within a residence hall room. This is so because those who talk loudly under the circumstances "cannot really be believed to have an expectation of privacy" (*People*, 1982, p. 610). Likewise, if you (or even a police officer) are properly within a student's room (e.g., with the student's consent, or incident to a lawful arrest) you may seize incriminating evidence or contraband which is in "plain view" (*Washington*, 1982; *State*, 1980a; *State*, 1976). Once the material is lawfully seized, it may be examined by an expert (*People*, 1971) or photocopied (*Stranhan*, 1982) and introduced into evidence at a campus disciplinary hearing or in a criminal trial. Different standards will apply, however, if government officials open a "sealed package" to examine its contents (*Walter*, 1980).

The "plain view" doctrine is only one example of the fact that a student is not considered to have a privacy right in matters which he or she knowingly exposes to the public. The same principle applies if property or premises have been abandoned (*Abel*, 1960); or if an individual voluntarily turns over certain information to a third party which the third party conveys to the government, e.g., the telephone company informs the police of the numbers dialed from a particular telephone (*Smith*, 1979). In any event, even if a student is held to have a justifiable expectation of privacy in what was discovered, there are a number of important exceptions to the general requirement that searches be conducted pursuant to a warrant.

Warrantless Searches

The Supreme Court has held that only "unreasonable" searches conducted without a warrant are condemned by the first clause of the Fourth Amendment. In determining what is a "reasonable" warrantless search, the Court has permitted the law to evolve "in light of contemporary norms and conditions" (*Payton*, 1980, p. 591). Generally, a warrantless search will be permitted for any of the following reasons: (1) in an emergency; (2) to inventory lawfully obtained material; (3) if effective consent is given; (4) for certain limited kinds of health and safety inspections; (5) in instances when the search is conducted solely to maintain discipline or security in a state agency or institution; (6) in certain vehicle searches; (7) incident to a lawful arrest, or when other forms of "immediate action" by law enforcement authorities are justified. Except for the latter two, all of these warrantless searches may occasionally be relied upon by your residence hall staff in the normal course of their duties.

Emergencies

One of the most important exceptions to the warrant requirement in the college and university setting is the search undertaken in response to an emergency. This exception is best demonstrated by *People*, (1971). In that case, a university employee smelled a "noxious odor" emanating from somewhere in a study hall. He used his master key to open over forty student lockers until he located a briefcase containing packets of marijuana which had been treated with a foul smelling preservative. The California Supreme Court held that the warrantless search was proper since the "malodorous smell permeating the entire study hall" required a "prompt inspection" for the purpose of "abating the nuisance" (p. 300).

The *People* case also indicates that it may be reasonable to examine the contents of a legally seized container or package in emergency situations, or if the contents are in "plain sight." Similarly, state officials may conduct a legitimate "inventory" search of items which are lawfully in their possession. For example, in *State* (1975), a junior college student left her purse in a classroom. The purse was eventually turned over to a campus security officer, who examined the contents and found amphetamines. The court held that the search was proper since the officer had lawful custody and "acted in good faith in conducting the inventory so as not to use it as a subterfuge for warrantless search" (p. 911). Even though the officer found Ms. Johnson's identification before he found the amphetamines, it was permissible for him to conduct a thorough inventory search in order to identify and "safeguard" her valuables. The contraband was then seized under the "plain view" doctrine (see *United States*, 1982).

Consent

Another significant exception to the warrant requirement is the "consent" search. It is important to understand, however, that valid consent must be specific, unequivocal, and truly voluntary (*Morale*, 1976; *Piazzola*, 1971). The contention that students who sign a residence hall contract give "implied" consent to any kind of a search would be viewed with suspicion by the courts, and could not be relied upon by law enforcement authorities (*Commonwealth*, 1970; *People*, 1968). Furthermore, although one student living in a room could consent to a search of the entire room, such consent would not routinely apply to the personal effects of another occupant (LaFave, 1980).

23

Health and Safety Inspections

Perhaps the most tenuous of the permissible warrantless searches is the "nonemergency" administrative health and safety inspection (see Warren, 1982, pp. 459-468). Although a number of lower courts have suggested that college and university officials may conduct health and safety inspections without a warrant (*Morale*, 1976; *State*, 1976), the Supreme Court has expressly held that comparable "fire, health, and housing code inspection programs" in the larger community, require the issuance of a warrant after "individualized review" by a "disinterested party" (*Camara*, 1967, p. 532). The Court recently reaffirmed this result in *Marshall*, (1978a) and has permitted deviations from it only in unique circumstances, such as warrantless searches of coal mines pursuant to the Federal Mine Safety and Health Act (*Donovan*, 1981).

Most college and university housing administrators are understandably reluctant to seek a warrant from a magistrate before undertaking a health and safety inspection. Accordingly, in order to limit the potential impact of *Camara* on public campuses, it would be prudent to have students give specific consent to such inspections in advance, perhaps in the residence hall contract. The inspections might be announced beforehand, or conducted on a routine schedule known to students, and should be limited in purpose and scope. Unannounced health and safety inspections, not authorized in the residence hall contract, could also be conducted if students consented to them at the time. If a student refused to give consent, it is conceivable that the courts might permit a college or university to rely upon an "internal" warrant procedure (e.g., a narrowly drawn search authorization, signed by a campus executive officer, see *Smyth*, 1975).

Maintaining Order and Discipline

Finally, a warrantless search which is occasionally relied upon by school officials is the administrative search to maintain security or discipline. This category of search was outlined in *Moore* (1968). The Court in that case upheld a warrantless search of a residence hall room by a campus administrator who was looking for drugs. It was held that:

> [t]he constitutional boundaryline between the right of the school authorities to search and the right of a dormitory student to privacy must be based on a reasonable belief on the part of the college authorities that a student is using a dormitory room for a purpose which is illegal or which would otherwise seriously interfere with campus discipline . . . . This standard of 'reasonable cause to believe' to justify a search by college administrators . . . is lower than the constitutionally protected criminal law standard of 'probable cause.' (p. 730)

The broad language used to permit the warrantless search in *Moore* (see also *United States*, 1969 and *Keene*, 1970) has been refined and narrowed in subsequent cases. In *Piazzola* (1971), the Court concluded that school regulations authorizing warrantless searches and seizures in a residence hall could not be used to justify a criminal conviction for possession of marijuana. It was held that the regulation in question could only be applied "to further the University's function as an educational institution" (p. 289). Similarly, in *Morale*, (1976) the Court determined that a "[warrantless] check or search of student's dormitory room is unreasonable under the Fourth Amendment unless [the institution] can show that the search furthers its functioning as an educational institution" (p. 998). Conducting a search for stolen property did not qualify under that standard, since "[t]he presence or absence of stealing on a campus does not disturb or disrupt the operation of its academic functions" (p. 998). Taken literally, this holding, and the holding in *Piazzola*, would limit warrantless searches designed to enforce campus disciplinary regulations to a very narrow range of cases involving disruption of the academic environment, damage to university property, academic fraud, and the like.

Exclusionary Rule

The various definitions of a "search" and the categories of permissible warrantless searches can be complicated and confusing. This problem is compounded by the fact that the courts are divided on the issue of what remedies may be available to students whose Fourth Amendment rights have been violated. It is true that students may be entitled to money damages in certain egregious cases, such as an unjustified "strip search" (*Doe*, 1980), or for violations of unquestioned Fourth Amendment rights (see, generally, *Wood*, 1975). What is unclear is whether the fruits of an unlawful search conducted by a public college official or law enforcement authority may be used as evidence in campus disciplinary proceedings.

Defendants in criminal cases may rely upon a judicially imposed "exclusionary rule" to suppress illegally seized evidence in certain cases. The exclusionary rule is designed to preserve the integrity of the judicial process and to deter law enforcement authorities from engaging in lawless behavior (*United States*, 1980b). Other free societies do not follow the rule (Wilson, 1981) and it has engendered considerable debate between reasonable and articulate commentators on both sides of the question (La Fave, 1982 and Oaks, 1970). In recent years, the Supreme Court has limited the applicability of the exclusionary rule (see, e.g., *United States*, 1980b; *Rakas*, 1978; *United States*, 1974) and, with the appointment of Justice O'Connor, it is likely that a majority on the Court now disapproves of it in its present form (LaFave, 1982). Furthermore, the United States Court of Appeals for the Fifth Circuit recently adopted a "good faith" exception to the rule (*State*, 1980), which has also been endorsed by a federal advisory panel.

Some courts have applied the exclusionary rule on campus (*Smyth*, 1975). In most cases, however, it has been held that illegally seized evidence may be considered in college and university disciplinary hearings, since the "Supreme Court clearly intends to limit the exclusionary rule . . . and to allow only a criminal defendant to invoke its protections" (*Morale*, 1976, p.1001). This reasoning has also been followed in the analogous setting of attorney disciplinary proceedings (*People*, 1981).

The fact that most courts do not require colleges and universities to adhere to the exclusionary rule in disciplinary hearings does not mean that institutional officials are precluded from doing so as a matter of policy. At campuses where there is ineffective supervision and control over those who enforce regulations, the administrative adoption of an exclusionary rule might be necessary in order to prevent a pattern of violations of student Fourth Amendment rights. Generally, however, the indiscriminate application of the exclusionary rule in the educational setting should be avoided, since it would produce unnecessary proceduralism in hearings which are designed, in part, to teach students that they are accountable for their actions.

Summary

1. Students have a legitimate right to privacy in their residence hall rooms.
2. It is not considered a "search" for a school official who has a right to be in a certain location to detect something by one of his natural senses.
3. Housing administrators may make reasonable warrantless searches in emergencies, for necessary maintenance, inventory, health and safety inspections, or to enforce appropriate regulations which further the educational mission of the institution. These searches should be undertaken with student consent whenever possible and should be limited in frequency and scope.
4. Generally, one student cannot legally consent to a search of the personal effects of another student, even if both occupy the same room.
5. Except in certain emergency situations, officials conducting a warrantless search should give notice of their identity and purpose, and should provide students with a written justification for the search.
6. Searches conducted for the purpose of initiating criminal prosecution, or which are likely to produce evidence of a crime, should be left to law enforcement officers.
7. Most courts do not preclude the consideration of illegally seized evidence in campus disiplinary proceedings. Some institutions may wish to do so as a matter of policy.

THE FOURTEENTH AMENDMENT

The Fourteenth Amendment states, in part, that:

All persons born or naturalized in the United States, and subject to the jurisdiction thereof, are citizens of the United States and of the State wherein they reside. No State shall make or enforce any law which shall abridge the privileges or immunities of citizens of the United States; nor shall any State deprive any person of life, liberty, or property, without due process of law; nor deny to any person within its jurisdiction the equal protection of the laws.

Originally, the framers of the Fourteenth Amendment were concerned about the rights of black people in the Southern courts after the civil war. As a result, the due process clause was designed to insure that persons could not be deprived of their life, their personal liberty, or their property as a penalty for a crime, without a fair trial (Berger, 1977). Over the years, however the terms "liberty" and "property" have been broadly defined by the courts to include a "liberty interest" in one's good name and reputation (*Wisconsin*, 1971) or a "property interest" in certain benefits provided by the state, such as free public education for elementary or high school students (*Goss*, 1975). Furthermore, the "due process" requirement has been applied to state proceedings other than criminal trials, including college and university disciplinary cases (*Dixon*, 1961).

The Fourteenth Amendment is specifically restricted to state action. Consequently, in the residence hall setting a student at a private school would not normally be entitled to constitutional due process protection prior to being removed from the halls on disciplinary or any other grounds (*Miller*, 1976). A student at a state school, however, could reasonably contend that such a dismissal would constitute a deprivation of a "property" right, based upon "the existence of rules and understandings promulgated and fostered by state officials . . ." (*Perry*, 1972, p. 602). Furthermore, although the case law is unclear at present, such a dismissal might also constitute an infringement of the student's "liberty" interest in his good name and reputation. The latter interest could be implicated even if the student was simply placed on official "probation" or otherwise had a finding of some sort of wrongdoing placed in his education records (*De Prima*, 1977; but see *Bishop*, 1976). In any event, if a property right or a liberty interest were infringed, the student would be entitled to some form of "due process."

The Process That's Due

Due process does not guarantee any specific type of procedure (*Cafeteria Workers*, 1961). Instead, the courts will balance the seriousness of the possible punishment against the risk of an erroneous determination and the fiscal and administrative burdens involved in offering various procedural protections (*Mathews*, 1976). Generally, in cases of student misconduct, the amount of "due process" should be in proportion to the penalty which might be imposed. For example, a student accused of participating in a minor prank in a residence hall might be in jeopardy of being placed on residence hall probation, required to make a small contribution to a local charity, complete a campus service project, or the like. All the due process that would be necessary under these circumstances would be "oral or written notice of the charges against him and, if he denies them, an explanation of the evidence the authorities have and an opportunity to present his side of the story" in an informal "discussion" with a school official (*Goss*, 1975, p. 581). The rationale for this common sense approach was best expressed by a federal judge in Kentucky, who recently observed that if educators have to make "a federal case out of every petty disciplinary incident, the whole purpose of having any discipline at all and any rules of conduct would be defeated" (*Bahr*, 1982, p. 487).

Students at tax-supported institutions who are subject to expulsion, lengthy suspension, dismissal from housing, significant financial penalties, or a lasting stigma (e.g. transcript notation of disciplinary action) will be entitled to more than rudimentary due process protection. Even in these cases, however, a "formal hearing in the true adversary context" is not required (*Whiteside*, 1978, p. 720). The courts recognize that disciplinary determinations made in the college and university setting should be distinguished from the imposition of criminal sanctions. It is understood and expected that campus administrators will use college regulations as a starting point for discussions with students about ethical issues. The punishments which may then be administered are designed, in part, to teach students that they are accountable for their actions. Most courts will be unwilling to impose a "criminal justice" model on campus as long as college and university officials understand the educational implications involved in such a process (*Zanders*, 1968).

The basic due process protections which are required in serious disciplinary cases at public institutions have been outlined in holdings such as *Dixon* (1961), *Esteban* (1967), *Morale* (1976), and in a Missouri federal court "General Order" (1968). Most recently, in *Sohmer* (1982), a federal district court reiterated that students must be given advance notice of the grounds of the charges against them; that they should be heard in their own defense; that they are to be provided with "the names and a summary of the testimony" of potential witnesses, even though they "may not be necessarily entitled to be confronted by the witnesses at the hearing;" and finally, that any disciplinary action be "based upon substantial evidence" (p. 53).

Disciplinary Hearings

In conducting disciplinary hearings you will encounter a number of issues which are not resolved in *Sohmer* or in those judicial decisions which set forth general due process standards. Additional guidance can be found in other relevant cases, as follows:

1. Colleges and universities have "inherent authority to maintain order and to discipline students" without specifying every conceivable form of misconduct in advance (*Norton*, 1969, p. 200).

2. College officials are expected to make a reasonable effort to inform students about the general types of conduct which are prohibited. It will not be sufficient in this regard to develop regulations which simply prohibit "indiscriminate" behavior or which allow only "wholesome" activities. Language of that nature permits "different officials [to] attach different meanings to the words in an arbitrary and discriminatory manner" and would be unconstitutionally vague (*Shamloo*, 1980, p. 523).

3. Students who are entitled to a hearing should be given reasonable time to prepare a defense. One court has suggested that ten days notice would be sufficient (*Speake*, 1970). Students who pose an immediate threat to others may be subject to an interim suspension prior to the hearing (*Goss*, 1975).

4. A hearing may be conducted in the absence of a student who fails to appear after campus officials have made a reasonable effort to provide adequate advance notice of the hearing time, date, and location (*Wright*, 1968).

5. Hearings need not be delayed until after a student has been tried on any concurrent criminal charges (*Goldberg*, 1967; *Nzuve*, 1975).

6. None of the cases setting forth general due process requirements have indicated that students must be appointed to serve on disciplinary hearing panels. Nonetheless, many schools elect to do so as a matter of policy.

7. Individuals serving on disciplinary hearing panels need not be disqualified because they have a superficial knowledge of the background of the case, or because they may know the participants. The basic test is whether or not the panelists can "judge the case fairly and solely on the evidence presented . . ." (*Keene*, 1970, p. 222; see also *Jones*, 1968). However, hearing panelists should not have participated in investigating or prosecuting the case (*Marshall*, 1980).

8. The "beyond a reasonable doubt" standard of proof used in criminal cases need not be adopted in campus disciplinary proceedings. Instead, at least one court has held that a student's guilt should be established by "clear and convincing evidence" (*Smyth*, 1975, p. 799).

9. Circumstantial evidence may be used in criminal proceedings and in campus disciplinary cases (*McDonald*, 1974). Likewise, colleges are not required to exclude "hearsay" evidence, although

it would be unwise to base a finding of guilt on hearsay evidence alone (*Racine*, 1982). Most other technical rules of evidence are not applicable in campus disciplinary proceedings (*Goldberg*, 1967).

10. Students appearing before disciplinary panels may be directed to answer questions pertaining to the charges against them. Students who refuse to answer on the ground of the Fifth Amendment privilege may be informed that the hearing panel could draw negative inferences from their refusal which might result in the imposition of significant disciplinary sanctions. Several courts have held that the response of a student who then elected to answer could not be used against him in a criminal proceeding (*Goldberg*, 1967; *Furutani*, 1969; *Nzuve*, 1975).

11. Most courts have held that students have no due process right to representation by legal counsel, as long as the institution does not proceed through counsel. Students who have concurrent criminal charges pending against them, however, should be permitted to consult with counsel during their disciplinary hearings. The role of counsel may be limited to consultation (*Gabrilowitz*, 1978).

12. Cases need not be dismissed on the ground that school officials failed to give students "Miranda" warnings about the right to remain silent. The Miranda rule has not been extended to the educational setting (*Boynton*, 1982).

13. A student subject to a serious penalty should be permitted to confront and cross examine witnesses if the case will be decided on questions of credibility (*Blanton*, 1973).

14. Hearings in serious disciplinary cases should be tape recorded or transcribed. Furthermore, students who are found guilty of the charges against them should be given written reasons for such a determination (*Morale*, 1976).

15. Due process does not require that the decision of the hearing panel be unanimous. A simple majority vote would be sufficient (*Nzuve*, 1975).

16. A student who is found guilty of the charges should not be subject to an additional punishment simply for having pled innocent. However, a hearing panel may consider a pattern of lying and fabrication by the student at a hearing and may impose a more severe penalty as a result (*United States*, 1978). Likewise, a student who is found guilty of the charges and who refuses to cooperate with institutional officials by identifying other participants in the misbehavior could be subject to an added punishment (*Roberts*, 1980).

17. Colleges and universities may establish disciplinary panels which make recommendations to an administrative officer who would review the record and the findings before making a final determination. Due process, however, does not require a formal right of appeal (*Reetz*, 1903; *National Union of Marine Cooks*, 1954).

18. Finally, the courts will expect both state and private institutions to follow their own regulations (*Tedeschi*, 1980; *Clayton*, 1981). Occasional harmless errors may be permitted, but campus officials will have to show that the deviations did not deny students a fair hearing (*Turof*, 1981).

Psychiatric Withdrawals

The technical problems involved in conducting a hearing are not the only difficult due process questions you will encounter. One issue of special concern is the removal of students on "medical" or psychiatric grounds. The legal considerations involved in responding to students who appear to have a mental disorder are complex, and require comprehensive development elsewhere. Basically, you should be alerted to the fact that section 504 of the Rehabilitation Act of 1973 prevents unlawful discrimination against handicapped individuals, including individuals suffering from "any mental or psychological disorder" (45 *C.F.R.* 84.3 (j) (2) (i) (B)). This does not mean that a recipient college or university must ignore or excuse the behavioral manifestations resulting from such disorders. Section 504 was designed to prohibit the exclusion of a handicapped student only "if the person can successfully participate in the education program and complies with the rules of the college and if his or her behavior does not impede the performance of the other students" (45 *C.F.R.* 84, App. A). It does mean, however, that students subject to removal from school (or from the residence halls) on the ground that they have a "mental disorder" will be entitled to some sort of due process protection, as required both by the handicap regulations (45 *C.F.R.* 84.7 (b)) and, at state schools, by the Fourteenth Amendment (*Evans*, 1980; *Nancy P.*, 1981).

With very few exceptions, such as attempted suicide, you might find it preferable to rely on the disciplinary process if students engage in conduct which is disruptive or threatening to others. An important benefit associated with the imposition of discipline on campus is that the language used to define prohibited conduct can be relied upon to affirm a shared set of behavioral standards. Psychiatric withdrawals, however, are based on hidden (or unknown) value judgments disguised by "medical" language (Pavela, 1982). College and university administrators who frequently resort to psychiatric withdrawals may be avoiding the demanding task of articulating the ethical precepts which support the behavioral expectations of the academic community. As a result, both withdrawn students and the campus as a whole are left without sufficient moral guidance.

Some administrators believe it is necessary to have a psychiatric withdrawal policy in order to remove suicidal students from the institution. It would be unwise, however, to adopt a policy which required the automatic removal of all students who threatened to harm themselves. Suicidal behavior is not the inevitable result of a serious mental disorder (Scheidman and Mandelkorn, 1970), nor does it necessarily indicate that the student is unable to cope with academic stress (Bernard and Bernard, 1980). Instead, a primary cause of suicide appears to be social isolation (Alvarez, 1973). Educators should be willing to make a reasonable effort to counsel students in these circumstances, rather than simply withdrawing them from school on psychiatric grounds. The latter approach would "be isolating [the] individuals from their peer group . . . thus intensifying rather than alleviating their distress" (Bernard and Bernard, 1980, p. 111). In any event, campus officials should remember that they have additional responsibilities to attempt to secure prompt evaluation and treatment for suicidal students, and to alert law enforcement authorities immediately if a student threatens to harm any specific identifiable victim (Gehring, 1982).

Group Sanctions

The punishment of groups of students for the misbehavior of a few unidentified individuals also raises a number of difficult issues, especially since "[f]reedom from punishment in the absence of *personal* guilt is a fundamental concept in the American scheme of justice" (*St. Ann*, 1974, p. 245; see also *Kline*, 1982). Nonetheless, it is not inconceivable that the courts might permit such a policy in special circumstances. For example, in *Rose* (1982), the U.S. Court of Appeals for the First Circuit upheld a school board decision temporarily suspending certain school bus routes due to the disruptive conduct of a number of unidentified students. The Court observed that no "reputational" injury was involved; that the inconvenience suffered by the students and their parents was "hardly a 'grievous loss;'" and that "the Board here has held full hearings on its policy [and] has considered alternatives . . ." (p. 283).

The holding in *Rose* can easily be confined to primary and secondary schools, and to special problems associated with safety of children on school buses. In the college and university setting, other courts have sought to discredit "the probably objectionable" practice of seeking to penalize students who merely belonged to a group in which some individuals had engaged in misbehavior (*Blanton*, 1973, p. 381). Accordingly, a campus regulation permitting the imposition of penalties without ascertaining individual culpability will be subject to very close judicial scrutiny. Educators who believe that it is necessary to engage in such a practice will have a better chance of success if they can document that they have made a genuine effort to explore other alternatives. It would also be advisable to create some mechanism which would permit students who contend they were innocent of any wrongdoing, to meet individually with the decisionmaker in order to correct any factual errors or misunderstandings. Above all, the penalties imposed should be relatively minor, and must not be used to stigmatize students in ways which would affect their future career prospects.

Equal Protection

Finally, you need to be aware that the Equal Protection Clause of the Fourteenth Amendment has also been relied upon in a number of relevant cases at state colleges and universities. For the most part, equal protection issues arise when students contend that certain classifications developed by school officials (e.g., mandatory residence hall living for freshmen) are arbitrary or irrational. The courts are not generally receptive to such cases, unless some patent form of prohibited discrimination is involved.

The Equal Protection Clause was designed to prevent "invidious discrimination between persons in similar circumstances" (*Jones*, 1968, p. 203). However, in the absence of the infringement of a "fundamental right" (such as the right to vote), or use of a "suspect classification" (such as race), the courts will uphold a classification or distinction made by state officials "if any state of facts reasonably may be conceived to justify it" (*McGowan*, 1961, p. 426). Furthermore, if a classification is determined to have some reasonable basis, it will not be considered a denial of equal protection simply because the classification "is not made with mathematical nicety or because in practice it results in some inequality" (*Lindsley*, 1911, p. 78).

One example of the application of the Equal Protection Clause in the college and university setting is *Bynes* (1975). There, several married students at the Stony Brook campus of the State University of New York challenged a university policy which limited married student housing to couples without children. The University justified the policy on the grounds that the housing in question was not designed for family living, and that children would be endangered by the fire hazards associated with "makeshift cooking arrangements" and inadequate emergency exits. The court upheld the University's decision and observed that the question was "not whether mother or even the court knows what is best, but whether the University's decision . . . was . . . arbitrary or irrational" (p. 257). There was a rational basis, in the opinion of the Court, "for the University . . . to postpone the residence of children until such time, if ever, that it can provide the housing it (and not the parents) deems adequate" (p. 258).

Reasoning similar to that articulated by the court in *Bynes* has been applied in *Prostrollo* (1974). In that case, a number of students at the University of South Dakota contended that a school policy requiring all single freshman and sopohmores to live in university housing denied them equal protection of the laws. The Court disagreed, and observed that the regulation was rationally defensible on the ground that the residence hall environment was specifically designed to assist "younger students, and underclassmen in adjusting to college life" (p. 778). As in *Bynes*, and the vast majority of comparable equal protection cases, the Court deferred to the reasoned judgment of university officials and refused to disturb the "broad power" given them "to formulate and implement educational policy" (p. 782).

Equal protection issues also may arise in the context of student discipline at public institutions. The most likely complaint is that the punishments imposed for the same misbehavior are not uniformly applied to every guilty student. Once again, in the absence of some sort of arbitrary discrimination, a decision to punish some, but not all students in precisely the same way will be upheld if it is "reasonably and fairly made" (*Jones*, 1968, p. 203). Likewise, as in the larger society, it is not necessary to apprehend every wrongdoer before prosecuting those who have been caught (*Zanders*, 1968).

Summary

1. Students are entitled to some sort of "due process" protection prior to being deprived of a "liberty" or "property" interest by state officials.
2. Due process does not require any specific type of procedure. Generally, in cases of student misconduct, the amount of due process should be in proportion to the penalty which might be imposed.
3. Trial-type hearings incorporating technical rules of evidence, full participation by counsel, the "beyond a reasonable doubt" standard of proof, and the like, are not required on campus, even in cases which might result in suspension or expulsion.
4. Students at both public and private institutions will be entitled to some due process protection prior to being removed from school (or from the residence halls) for psychiatric reasons.
5. The punishment of groups of students for the misbehavior of a few unidentified individuals is legally questionable. Educators who believe it is necessary to engage in such a practice should impose only minor penalties which do not leave students with disciplinary records. It would also be advisable to create some mechanism which would allow students to establish that they were not participants in the prohibited activity.
6. The Equal Protection Clause of the Fourteenth Amendment protects students at state schools from "invidious discrimination." Nonetheless, the courts will uphold "reasonable" classifications made by campus officials even if those classifications are not formulated with mathematical precision.

References

Alvarez, A., *The savage god*. New York: Bantam, 1973.

Bernard, M. L. and Bernard, J. L., Institutional responses to the suicidal student: Ethical and legal considerations. *Journal of College Student Personnel*, 1980, 21, 109-113.

Berger, R., *Government by judiciary*. Cambridge: Harvard University Press, 1977.

Gehring, D., The counselors' "Duty to warn." *Personnel and Guidance Journal*, 1982, *61*(4), 208-210.

General order on judicial standards of procedure and substance in review of student discipline in tax supported institutions of higher education. 45 *F.R.D.* 133 (W.D. Mo., 1968).

Kaplin, W. A., *The law of higher education*, San Francisco: Jossey-Bass, 1978.

LaFave, W. R. and Israel, J. H., *Criminal procedure: Constitutional limitations*, St Paul: West Publishing Company, 1980.

LaFave, W. F., The fourth amendment in an imperfect world: On drawing "Bright Lines" and "Good Faith," *University of Pittsburgh Law Review*, 1982, 43, 307-361.

Neely, R. N., *How courts govern America*, New Haven: Yale University Press, 1981.

New York Times, Panel on violent crime urges relaxation of evidence rules, August 6, 1981, p. A12.

Oaks, D. H., Studying the exclusionary rule in search and seizure, *University of Chicago Law Review*, 1970, 37, 665-757.

Pavela, G., Therapeutic paternalism and the misuse of mandatory psychiatric withdrawals on campus, *The Journal of College and University Law*, 1982, 9, 101-141.

Report of the committee on freedom of expression at Yale University, New Haven: Yale University, 1975. Cited in the *New York Times*, January 26, 1975, p. 18.

Shneidman, E. S. and Mandelkorn, P. How to prevent suicide. In Shneidman (Ed.), *The Psychology of Suicide*, New York, 1970.

Stevens, G. E., Faculty Tort liability for libelous student publications, *Journal of Law and Education*, 1976, 5, 307-316.

Thigpen, R., The application of fourteenth amendment norms to private colleges and universities , *Journal of Law and Education.* 1982, 11, 171-208.

Warren, K F., *Administrative law*, St. Paul: West Publishing Company, 1982.

Wilson, J. O., The evidence is in—can we use it? *Washington Post*, October 21, 1981 p. A.27.

Chapter III

Statutes and Regulations Affecting Residence Hall Operations and Staff

Donald D. Gehring

The constitutional issues referred to in the previous chapter outline only one of the relationships you have with students and staff. There are several other legal relationships which define the interplay between the rights and responsibilities of the institution, students, and the staff. The statutes or laws of your state and federal government also create certain rights and impose certain duties. As an official of your institution it is implicitly expected that you will abide by all applicable federal and state laws. Your housing operation is also implicitly expected to be in conformity with applicable law. Failure to comply with applicable statutory provisions, either federal or state, could result in criminal charges or civil liability.

State and federal laws may not restrict rights guaranteed by the U.S. and state Constitutions; however, they may set standards higher than those imposed by the Constitution. For example, a curfew for women students, imposed by Eastern Kentucky University, was shown not to violate the Equal Protection Clause of the Fourteenth Amendment to the United States Constitution (*Robinson*, 1973). However, a curfew imposed only upon women students probably would constitute a violation of Title IX (a federal law) since that Act sets a higher standard than does the Fourteenth Amendment. Yet, Title IX is not in conflict with the Fourteenth Amendment.

STATE STATUTES

The laws of each state are different. No two states will have exactly the same laws, and even similar laws may be interpreted differently. You should, therefore, become familiar with the laws in the particular state in which you are employed. The most obvious example of the difference between state laws is the legal age for consumption of alcholic beverages. Not only will the age differ from state to state but the interpretation of the word "alcoholic beverage" may also be different. In one state, a student who is eighteen years old might be able to drink only beer and wine. However, the same student might legally be able to consume hard liquor by driving across the line to the neighboring state. A good listing of the state laws pertaining to alcoholic beverages was published in the *ACUHO NEWS*, (1981).

State laws are published in a set of volumes and generally have an index(es). These publications are often annotated and provide interpretations of the specific law. Looking in the index under key words can be helpful in gaining an insight into the laws of your state. Since there is so much variance between the laws of different states, there is no way to cover them in this monograph. The key words listed below, however, may be of help in locating laws in the index of your state code which impinge upon your daily operations.

Key Words

Age of Majority	Indemnification
Alcoholic Beverages	Landlord-Tenant
Bonds	Liability
Colleges and Universities	Negligence
Communications, Privileged	Property or Real Property
Contracts	Records
Contributory Negligence	Schools and Colleges
Dramshop	Search/Seizure
Drugs	Students
Facilities	Teachers
Fraternities and Sororities	Theft
Hazing	Torts
Higher Education	Universities
Higher Education Facilities	Weapons

FEDERAL LAWS

The United States Constitution is the supreme law of the land and the federal government can not enact laws which exceed the authority granted to it by the Constitution. Two powers granted to the federal government form the basis for most of the federal laws pertaining to higher education—the regulation of interstate commerce and funding to maintain the general welfare. Once a law is enacted (legislative function) the appropriate executive agencies will issue regulations to effectuate the law (executive branch function) and if a controversy arises, the judicial branch of government fulfills its function by providing an interpretation of the law. As an administrator, responsible for the operation of housing on the campus, you should know all three aspects—the law, its implementing regulations, and judicial interpretations.

There have been federal laws affecting institutions of higher education since before the Morrill Act of 1862. Some federal laws have an indirect impact on the operation of your institution while others are designed to apply specifically to your college or university. The Age Discrimination in Employment Act of 1967 (29 *U.S.C.* 621) prohibits employment discrimination against individuals between age 40 and 65. The Act was not designed to apply specifically to colleges and universities; however, since the Act covers employers with twenty or more employees, colleges and universities would fall within its scope. On the other hand, Title IX of the Education Amendments of 1972 (20 *U.S.C.* 1681) was designed to apply specifically to educational institutions and prohibits discrimination on the basis of sex, *in educational programs or activities.* These examples also illustrate the point that some federal laws are designed to apply primarily to staff, while others are designed to apply primarily to students.

In addition to laws which apply to your students and staff, there are also statutes regulating your use of copyrighted materials, the protection of human subjects (even in psychological research), occupational health and safety, and others. There are volumes written on these laws and regulations and while they are beyond the scope of this chapter, several of the more sigificant statutes are listed in Appendix C. These laws, although not discussed here, are important and do impact your daily operations. Often the requirements of these laws are implemented and monitored by some other agency on campus. However, you should do your own follow-up study of these statutes in order to become familiar with their requirements. In this way you will be better able to make housing decisions within the context of the whole institution.

The remainder of this chapter is organized into two sections— federal laws pertaining to students, and those pertaining to employees. The statutes discussed are those which most directly impinge upon your work with students and staff. Several other laws which impact students and employees, not discussed here, are listed in Appendix C.

Federal Laws Affecting Students
Title VI

The civil rights movement of the 1960's produced a significant piece of legislation designed to end racial discrimination in our society. The Civil Rights Act of 1964 included, as one of its parts, Title VI. This law states:

> No person in the United States shall, on the ground of race, color, or national origin, be excluded from participation in, be denied the benefits of, or be subjected to discrimination under any program or activity receiving federal financial assistance (42 *U.S.C.* 2000(d)).

Under Title VI, an institution is considered to receive federal financial assistance, and therefore comes under the prohibitions of Title

VI, if one student attends the institution using veterans benefits (*Bob Jones*, 1974). If your institution has students receiving G.I. benefits or other federal financial assistance, whether you are public or private, you are probably required to comply with Title VI.

The most famous case involving Title VI is the *Bakke* decision (1978). The Supreme Court held in *Bakke* that while race or national ancestry may be considered as a *factor* in the admissions process, it may not be used as the *exclusive criteria*. In *Bakke* a quota was established for minority students in the first-year class of a medical school. Thus, non-minority students were excluded, on the basis of race, from competing for those reserved spaces, and this was held to violate Title VI. The same reasoning would apply to campus housing. Facilities which restrict occupancy on the basis of race would violate the prohibitions of Title VI.

Campus regulations at one school requiring that black students must serve on two of the governing bodies of the student council, were also found to violate Title VI (*Uzzell*, 1979). A similar finding was made with respect to a financial aid program where a specific percentage of financial aid was reserved for minority students (*Flanagan*, 1976). The point to be made is that programs or activities which exclude anyone on the basis of race, color, or national origin would violate Title VI. The exclusion need not be total exclusion, but may be created through the establishment of a quota, as in the cases described above. A special floor in the residence hall, restricted to students of a particular ethnic minority or nationality, would probably be held to be illegal even though every other floor is open to all students.

Your institution also executed a compliance statement for Title VI. This statement was most likely signed by your president and states that your institution will comply with Title VI, and its implementing regulations (34 *C.F.R.* 100). This compliance statement gives the Office of Civil Rigthts almost blanket permission to obtain information from your institution—even in areas which do not receive federal financial assistance (*United States*, 1979).

The penalty for failing to comply with Title VI could be a loss of federal funds.

Title IX

The Education Amendments of 1972 contains the now famous Title IX, which prohibits discrimination on the basis of sex (20 *U.S.C.* 1681). This law is modeled after Title VI and uses almost the exact same language.

No person in the United States shall, on the basis of sex, be excluded from participation in, be denied the benefits of, or be subjected to discrimination under any educational program or activity receiving federal financial assistance. (20 *U.S.C.* 1681).

As a housing administrator you should also know that the law specifically states:

Notwithstanding anything to the contrary contained in this title, nothing contained herein shall be construed to prohibit any educational institution receiving funds under this Act, from maintaining separate living facilites for the different sexes. (20 *U.S.C.* 1686)

Since Title IX is modeled after Title VI, a "recipient" of federal financial assistance would be similarly defined for both statutes (*Grove City College*, 1982). The same enforcement scheme is also used for both laws, with the primary mechanism being the loss of federal aid; although a private remedy also exists (*Cannon*, 1979). However, the funding can only be terminated in the ". . . particular program or part thereof, in which such noncompliance has been so found" (34 *C.F.R.* 100.8(c); *North Haven Board of Education*, 1982). If there is no direct federal aid to the institution, noncompliance can result in a loss of federal aid to students (*Grove City College*, 1982).

As with Title VI, your institution was required to sign a statement that gives the government the authority to inspect your records to ensure compliance.

As you have probably noticed, Title IX is a very broad statement. The real meat of the law is found in the regulations designed to effectuate it. It is these regulations that you need to be most familiar with. The regulations can be found at 34 *C.F.R.* 106.

Almost every section of the Title IX regulations can affect your daily housing operation—recruitment of staff; financial assistance; counseling and counseling or appraisal materials; access to course offerings; rules and regulations; services; full-time and student employment, including compensation; fringe benefits, and job structure and classification; and health and insurance benefits and services. Thus, it's important that you read the regulations and review the self-study of your housing operation. The self-study was a requirement under the law. These peripheral areas may not have received much attention when the self-study was conducted.

The regulations also contain a specific section on "Housing" (34 *C.F.R.* 106.32) and another on "Comparable Facilities," (34 *C.F.R.* 106.33). The "Housing" section includes references to fees, rules and regulations, policies and practices, as well as providing living arrangements which are *comparable* in quality and cost for members of both sexes. The "Housing" section also specifies that you must take reasonable steps to assure yourself that *off-campus listings* are comparable in quality and cost, and proportionately provided to members of both sexes.

What constitutes comparable facilities, in terms of both quality and cost, may not be easy to determine. The reasonableness standard would probably apply. However, it would most likely not be considered reasonable to provide single rooms only for members of one sex. The requirement to take reasonable steps to assure comparability in off-campus housing, only applies if you provide listings, or in any other way assist in making off-campus housing available to your students. Not only must you take steps to assure comparable off-campus accommodations are provided, but you must also take steps to assure that the quantity of such accommodations are proportionately provided to both sexes. This proportion would be based upon the number of students seeking off-campus living arrangements.

Hall Directors, R.A.'s and Hall Councils need to be especially aware of the prohibitions in Title IX which apply to rules and regulations. Rules designed only to apply to members of one sex would violate the law. Similarly, disciplinary sanctions applied only to members of one sex, are also prohibited (34 *C.F.R.* 106.31(b)(4)). Nor may any sex based requirements be placed on students as a prerequisite for being housed, applying for specific types of housing, or enjoying any other benefits or services provided by the University.

Section 504

The Rehabilitation Act of 1973 also contains a section related to educational programs and activities. Section 504 (29 *U.S.C.* 794), as it is popularly known, is also modeled after Title VI. Thus, a "recipient" institution would be defined in the same way. Since almost every institution has students attending who receive some form of federal aid, this law, as well as the others mentioned above, probably applies to your college or university. Compliance assurances and a self-study are required under 504 also. The intent of Section 504 is to eliminate discrimination on the basis of handicap. Specifically the law states:

No otherwise qualified handicapped individual . . . shall solely by reason of his handicap, be excluded from the participation in, be denied the benefits of, or be subjected to discrimination under any program or activity receiving federal financial assistance . . .. (29 *U.S.C.* 794).

There are some important distinctions to be made between Section 504 and Titles VI and IX. Section 504 prohibits discrimination against "otherwise qualified" handicapped individuals. Individuals are "otherwise qualified" if they are able to meet the requirements established in spite of their handicap (*Southeastern Community College*, 1979). Reasonable accomodations by the institution might be required however, in academic programs or work situations.

The definition of handicapped individuals is also important to understand, since it includes persons who have physical or mental impairments which substantially limit a major life activity, or persons who have a record of such impairments, and even those who are regarded as having such an impairment. Drug addicts and alcoholics are included as handicapped individuals (34 *C.F.R.* 104.3). Students with mental impairments are also considered handicapped. If they are admitted to the institution, then you must offer them housing on the same basis as the other students. If handicapped students create behavioral problems in the residence halls, you may discipline them just as you would any other student, so long as you do so evenly with respect to all students.

Section 504 cases which have received the most publicity are those dealing with admissions (*Southeastern Community College*, 1979), re-admission (*Doe*, 1981), and providing interpreter services (*Jones*, 1982). These cases are certainly of interest, but as a housing administrator you are more directly concerned with the accessibility of facilities, the specific housing regulations and the operation of student programs in the halls.

Only facilities where construction began after the effective date, must be accessible. Also, buildings altered after the effective date must be accessible. The effective date of the regulations (34 *C.F.R.* 104) was June 3, 1977. To determine accessibility, the standards of the American National Standards Institute (ANSI) will be used. Facilities not in compliance with ANSI standards are acceptable if equivalent access is provided.

While Section 504 does not require buildings built prior to the effective date to be accessible, it does require all programs to be accessible to handicapped students. In addition, the rules also specifically state that if you provide housing to nonhandicapped students you must now (since June 3, 1980) provide housing to handicapped students ". . . in sufficient quantity and variety so that the scope of handicapped students'choice of living accommodations is, as a whole comparable to that of nonhandicapped students" (34 *C.F.R.* 104.45(a)). Like Title IX, the housing section of the 504 regulations also specifies that you must assure yourself that *off-campus accommodations* are, on the whole, provided without discrimination (34 *C.F.R.* 104.45(b)).

Program accessibility is the primary aim of Section 504. This means that the programs you operate in housing must be available to "otherwise qualified" handicapped students. Care should be exercised when a determination is being made whether a particular handicapped student is "otherwise qualified." Columbia University was held to have violated Section 504 regulations by refusing to allow a student to participate in intercollegiate football because the student was only sighted in one eye (*Wright*, 1981).

The self-study required by the Act would be a good place to begin to determine if you are in compliance. This document should be available and you can use it to determine if anything has changed or if facilities, added or renovated since the study was completed, are in compliance.

The Family Educational Rights and Privacy Act of 1974

The Buckley Amendment (20 *U.S.C.* 1232 g) is the popular name for this piece of legislation which is sometimes also referred to by its accronym FERPA. The Amendment (because it was an amendment to another Act) differs from the previous laws discussed. Rather than prohibiting discrimination on the basis of a particular quality, FERPA protects the privacy of students' records and generally allows students the right of access to those records. The rights granted under this law apply to any postsecondary student, regardless of age.

The law applies to any college or university which receives funds directly from the Office of Education, or which has students in attendance who receive work-study funds, Pell grants, National Direct Student Loans, Guaranteed Student Loans or Supplemental Opportunity Grants.

The implementing regulations (34 *C.F.R.* 99) require that your institution adopt a Buckley Amendment policy which generally informs students of their rights under the law, including such items as procedures to be followed in requesting an inspection of records and cost of copies; definitions of "school officials" and "legitimate educational interests," among other things. Students must be notified annually of where this policy may be obtained and their right to file complaints.

The records to which the law applies are any records kept by the institution or those persons acting for the institution, which are directly related to the student. While that includes almost every record kept, there are some important distinctions to be made in this regard.

An individual does not become a student until the individual is in attendance (34 *C.F.R.* 99.3). Thus, an individual who has applied, but is not yet in attendance, does not have a right to inspect the housing file you may have developed with reference to them. You may also disclose "directory information" without a student's signed written consent. This information might include such items as name, room number, telephone number, major, dates of attendance and other such demographic data. However, this information must be listed in your institution's policy. In addition, the student must be informed of what information will be divulged and be given an opportunity to refuse to permit disclosure of any or all items of directory information (34 *C.F.R.* 99.3). Obviously, its not a good idea to give out any information on the telephone.

Of particular concern to housing administrators is the exception provided for "personal notes." These types of anecdotal notes, often kept by R.A.'s or Hall Directors, are exempt from student inspection if they are only kept by the individual RA or Director and never shared with anyone else except a short term substitute (34 *C.F.R.* 99.3(b)(1)(i)-(ii)). Housing officials may also be particularly interested in the

44

disclosure exceptions as they relate to parents. Information may be divulged to the parents of financially dependent students (as defined by the I.R.S.) without the students' consent (34 *C.F.R.* 99.31(a)(8)). Information pertaining to a specific student may also be disclosed, without the student's consent, in a health or safety emergency (34 *C.F.R.* 99.31(a)(10)).

Since the law was designed to protect the privacy of student records, judicial hearings must be closed. The student can waive this or any other right under the Act, however. It would be useless to protect the privacy of a students' records if everyone on campus were allowed to attend the hearing at which the record was being developed (Marston, 1976).

Finally, it is important to understand that this law applies to students but not to employees. You may, however, have a state law which provides for the protection of records of public employees. If a student is an employee, the employment records of the student are not covered by the Act; but the act does apply to all the *educational records* of the student employee (34 *C.F.R.* 99.3(3)(i)-(ii)).

FEDERAL LAWS AFFECTING EMPLOYEES

There are many federal laws which protect employees. While it is important to be familiar with all of these, only a few will be discussed here. Several laws not discussed here, are listed in Appendix C for further study.

Executive Order 11246 as Amended

Any institution which has federal contracts for more than $10,000 is covered under this order. The order sets forth the policy of the federal government to provide equal employment opportunity based on merit, and without discriminating on conditions of race, religion, sex, color or national origin. If your institution has federal contracts in excess of $50,000, then you would need to have an affirmative action plan and an affirmative action officer. Generally there must be an assessment of the work force conducted to determine if women and minorities are being "underutilized." Goals should then be set to overcome the underutilization and a timetable established within which the goals will be pursued. Recognize that goals and quotas are not the same thing.

The Executive Order and its amendments may be found at 30 *F.R.* 12319, 32 *F.R.* 14303, 41 *C.F.R.* 60-2, 41 *C.F.R.* 60, and 41 *F.R.* 29016.

Title VII

This federal law is probably the basis for more employee litigation than any other. It states that:

It shall be an unlawful employment practice for an employer—
(1) to fail or refuse to hire or to discharge any individual, or otherwise

to discriminate against any individual with respect to his compensation, terms, conditions, or privileges of employment, because of such individual's race, color, religion, sex, or national origin; or (2) to limit, segregate, or classify his employees or applicants for employment in any way which would deprive or tend to deprive any individual of employment opportunities or otherwise adversely affect his status as an employee, because of such individual's race, color, religion, sex, or national origin. (42 *U.S.C.* 2000e2)

Unlike the Executive Order, Title VII does not require that your institution have any federal contracts in order to be applicable. Title VII applies to every institution engaged in commerce, which has fifteen or more employees. Thus, it would seem to include all higher education institutions. The law created the Equal Employment Opportunity Commission (EEOC) to investigate complaints, attempt resolution, or initiate suit on behalf of the grieved employee. In addition to regular employees, students employed by your institution are also covered under Title VII.

Discrimination under Title VII can include working conditions as well as overt discriminatory acts. As a housing administrator, you need to be alert to this possibility since many housing employees are hired for "live in" positions. This type of discrimination was found at a junior high school where the womens' gym instructor was provided a small office with no private toilet or shower facility and the womens' gym had no natural light or ventilation. The male instructors had private facilities and their gym was definitely superior. The female gym teacher's Title VII suit alleging sex discrimination was successful and she was awarded compensatory damages and attorney's fees (*Harrington*, 1976).

Sexual harassment is also considered to constitute sexual discrimination under Title VII. The EEOC has issued guidelines which define sexual harassment in the following manner:

Unwelcome sexual advances, requests for sexual favors, and other verbal or physical conduct of a sexual nature constitute sexual harassment when (1) submission to such conduct is made either explicitly or implicitly a term or condition of a individual's employment; (2) submission to or rejection of such conduct by an individual is used as the basis for employment decisions affecting such individual; or (3) such conduct has the purpose or effect of reasonably interfering with an individual's work performance or creating an intimidating, hostile, or offensive working environment. (24 *C.F.R.* 1604(a))

You should also be aware that under these guidelines an employer can be held responsible for the acts of subordinates. In addition, you can be held responsible if you know that sexual harassment is taking place, even by a *non-employee*, and you fail ". . . to take immediate and appropriate corrective action" (24 *C.F.R.* 1604(e)). This type of situation might arise where students generate an "intimidating, hostile, or offensive working environment" for one of your staff, and after being notified of this situation, you fail to take corrective action. The guidelines set forth preventative steps that should be taken by employers, which include the establishment of a procedure to handle complaints.

Title IX

Subpart D of the Title IX regulations (34 *C.F.R.* 106.51) pertains specifically to sex discrimination in employment. The United States Supreme Court has held that the Title IX prohibition against sex discrimination in educational programs receiving federal funds, was also applicable to employees at recipient institutions (*North Haven Board of Education,* 1982). However, the Court pointed out that ". . . an agency's authority under Title IX both to promulgate regulations and to terminate funds is subject to the program specific limitation of 901 and 902" (p.4507). A subsequent decision by a federal district court used the Supreme Court's "program specific" test to deny the Department of Education the right to investigate Title IX complaints in an athletic department which received no direct federal aid (*University of Richmond,* 1982).

The employment aspects of the Title IX regulations (34 *C.F.R.* 106.61) cover recruitment, hiring practices, rates of pay, job assignments, leaves for pregnancy or child care (this applies to either the father or mother), fringe benefits, selection for attendance at conferences or related training, recreation programs or any other terms or conditions of employment. You are not permitted to make inquiries of an employment applicant's marital or parental status during a pre-employment interview nor make employment decisions based upon those factors.

The regulations do state that sex may be a bona fide occupational qualification if sex is ". . . essential to the successful operation of the employment function . . ." (34 *C.F.R.* 106.61). While the regulations do not specify a hall director's position in a single sex hall, they do cite two examples of employment in toilet or locker room facilities as positions justifying bona fide sex-related occupational qualifications. On this basis it may be safe to assume that a hall director's position in a single-sex hall would also qualify as a position justifying bona fide sex-related occupational qualifications.

Fair Labor Standards Act

This statute (29 *U.S.C.* 201) which requires payment of minimum wages, sets overtime rates, and establishes record keeping requirements has become very important for housing officials during the past few years. In *National League of Cities* (1976) the Supreme Court held that federal law could not impose minimum wage requirements on the states. Thus, state employees, including RA's and other housing officials at state institutions, are not covered by the minimum wage provisions of the F.L.S.A. However, most states have their own minimum wage laws and these statutes would apply to such state employees unless they were specifically exempted in the law.

The Fair Labor Standards Act (FLSA) does, however, apply to private colleges and universities. The Labor Department is the agency responsible for insuring compliance with the law. Based on charges brought by the Labor Department, a New York federal district court found undergraduate RA's at Marist College to be "employees" under the law and thus subject to all record keeping requirements, minimum wage, and overtime provisions of the law (*Marshall*, 1977). That 1977 decision was relied upon for several years.

In 1981, however, the Tenth Circuit Court of Appeals rendered a decision (*Marshall*, 1978) which held that students who perform the typical RA functions at private institutions were not *employees* for purposes of the F.L.S.A.. These RA's were provided a $1,000 tuition stipend, a reduced room rate, and a free telephone. In a footnote to the case the court said "Insofar as the facts of *Marist* are not clearly distinguishable from those presented in the instant case, we believe that *Marist* was wrongly decided" (p.9). The Labor Department did not appeal the decision, thus allowing it to stand.

In a subsequent decision in Idaho, a federal district court followed the precedent set in the Regis case by issuing a summary judgment favoring Northwest Nazarene College (*Donovan*, 1982). The Labor Department had attempted to classify RA's at Northwest Nazarene as "employees" subject to the F.L.S.A. minimum wage provisions.

MISCELLANEOUS FEDERAL LAWS

Cases involving two other federal laws related to housing-specific situations have also been decided recently. These cases do not involve the laws discussed above, but they do deserve mentioning.

While not involving a college or university, one case has obvious implications for housing "live-in" staff. The case involved an offshore oil rig and the value of room and board provided by the employer for the people employed on the rig (*Rowan Companies, Inc.*, 1981). The Internal Revenue Service attempted to tax the value of this room and board. The individuals who worked on the rig stayed there for several days at a time before being taken back to shore for a few days leave. The United States Supreme Court denied the IRS the right to tax the value and established the following test:

> . . . an employee may exclude from gross income the value of meals and lodging furnished to him by his employer if: the employer furnished both the meals and the lodging for its own convenience, fur-

nished the meals on its business premises, and requires the employee to accept the lodging on the business premises as a condition of employment. (4647)

The federal Fair Housing Act (42 *U.S.C.* 3601) has also been the basis for litigation which has an impact on the relationship between college housing operations and local landlords. In one instance several rental apartments were converted from open market facilities to housing exclusively for university students. A former tenant in the apartments claimed that the effect of this conversion was to deprive low income Black tenants of adequate housing (*Dreher*, 1980). No violation of the Fair Housing Act was found in this situation and the court said that "As long as their plan results in such a wholesale conversion, at the expense of the general population but in favor of the student population, no violation of applicable law is apparent" (p. 935).

The United States Justice Department also attempted to bring suit against Brigham Young University under the Fair Housing Act. Students at the University were only permitted to live in sex segregated off campus apartment buildings. The Department initially decided that this caused landlords to segregate their facilities in order to be eligible to house B.Y.U. students. The Department, however, reached an agreement with B.Y.U. and the practice was not found to violate the law (Oaks, 1978).

Summary
Relationships with students, staff, and agencies outside your institution are affected by state and federal laws and regulations. While some of these laws pertain specifically to educational institutions, others apply to your operation because you are an employer or engaged in commerce. An understanding of these laws and their implementing regulations is as important to your housing operation as a knowledge of good business practice or developmental theory. Your policies, practices, and procedures should be tested against applicable law. Effective decision making requires that you understand your rights and responsibilities, as well as those of your students and staff, as they are created by these laws. This chapter can provide a good beginning, but further study and consultation with counsel are necessary if you are to become familiar with the laws which impinge upon your daily housing operations.

References
Oaks, D., Personal Communication, March 15, 1978.

Legislative Issues and Information. *ACUHO NEWS*, 1981, 21 (3), p. 16.

Chapter IV

Contracts and Their Use in Housing

Stephen T. Miller

The Housing Contract is at the core of the relationship between residential students and the institution. It defines the rights and responsibilities for both parties, and places limits on what each can do and expect. Consequently, a well written housing contract is essential for the smooth operation of a housing department.

In broad terms, any contract is a three-party agreement. There are normally two parties involved in the contract itself, and the state as a third party, sets rules by which contracts must be made. Unlike issues of individual rights, a contract is a non-constitutional issue. It is a matter of civil law, with the rules set by the individual state. Thus, as a housing administrator you should become familiar with the law of contracts of your particular state.

Rules of contracts are set by the state legislature and interpreted by the courts. The actual rules of contracts are often quite similar between states. All states but Louisiana share an English Common Law background (*Uniform Commercial Code*, 1962). Consequently, their rules of contracts have developed from a similar source and are often much the same. Nonetheless, there are differences in detail that must be explored. No general presentation on contracts can cover these differences. The same general commentary can be applied to the courts when they interpret state contract law. Again, to facilitate the flow of commerce between states, similar rules are ofter interpreted the same. Still, there may be differences in detail, and individual work will be needed to track these down.

This is not to say that one state's decision has no impact on a sister state. While a ruling by a state court in Pennsylvania has no binding impact on a court in Colorado, the Colorado court may find Pennsylvania's ruling to be persuasive and adopt it when a similar situation arises in Colorado. Thus, while states are independent jurisdictions, they do rely upon one another for reasoning and logic. This means that housing administrators should be aware of what *trends* are occurring in other states, but should not be overly concerned by them until the question arises in his or her home state.

Given the above as a general overview, let's now look at the specific requirements for a contract, and basically how one should be drafted. Again, keep in mind that the general rules apply to everyone, but that each institution needs to develop a document which is specific to their needs.

WHAT IS A CONTRACT

Generally, the publication entitled, *Restatement of Contract* 2d, (1981) defines a contract as:

. . . A promise or a set of promises for the breach of which the law gives a remedy or the performance of which the law in some way recognizes as a duty. (p. 5)

This is a functional definition which is quite clear in its own terms. If two people exchange promises in an appropriate manner, they are presumed to have a contract. Should one refuse to perform, the other party could turn to the courts for redress.

Needless to say, if this were all that there was, contracts would be an obvious area of the law and no one would need to draw upon the courts for definition or help. This is not the case, and to better understand the actual workings of a contract we need to look at the separate pieces needed to put one together. Basically, we need: (1) a promise, or set of promises; (2) an offer and acceptance; (3) a bargained-for exchange and eventually; (4) a meeting of the minds. Given all of these, we have "consideration" and the basis of a contract. Let's examine each of these.

TYPES OF CONTRACTS AND THEIR ELEMENTS

As the *Restatement* (1981) points out, promises are the basic medium of exchange in a contract. A contract can be based on either a solitary promise, or a set of mutual promises. A solitary promise leads to a unilateral contract. This is the type of arrangement that flows from a reward, or an open request for services. If a school has a problem with false alarms in the residence halls, it is quite normal for a reward to be offered for the apprehension of the individual setting off the alarms. This, in essence, is a unilateral contract. It is a promise of reward made to the general public and not to someone in particular. No individual has been hired to solve the false alarm problem and no one has promised to do so. The only promise made is the one of reward, should certain events transpire. Thus, we have a solitary promise leading to a contract, once the requested actions have been completed (*Cook*, 1950). This would be a valid unilateral contract, and the reward must be paid once the individual setting off the alarms has been caught.

The more common type of contract is that of a promise made for a promise. This is called a "bilateral" contract. This is what happens when you order a new car, hire a painter to paint your house, or when a student signs a housing contract. Here the student promises to abide by the terms of agreement and to pay a stipulated rent. The institution also agrees to abide by the terms of the agreement and to make space available to the student for the purpose of housing.

The Promises

In essence, both parties are promising to do something. More than that, they are both promising to so something because the other is making certain promises. It is this exchange of promises that is the essence of the bilateral contract.

Thus a contract can be based upon either a solitary promise by one party, or on the mutual promises of all parties involved. In either case, the promise(s) becomes the foundation of any contract to come. However, before a contract is present, other issues must be considered.

A promise is in essence an offer. In *Lucy* (1954), the court looked at what may or may not be an offer. An offer was found to exist based upon the intent of the parties and the specific details involved. The same kind of analysis found no offer to be present in *Abrams* (1979). In the unilateral example, an offer of reward is made for a particular action. In the bilateral example, both promises are also offers. An offer of housing is made if certain moneys are paid and other conditions are met. The student, in turn, offers money for accommodations under certain conditions.

A contractual offer does basically two things. First, it stipulates what is to be had, and under what conditions. Second, it extends a grant of power to the other party involved. In effect, it says you can bind me to this offer under the terms given, should you care to accept it.

The person making the offer shares the power to be given, by making stipulations. First there are the specifics of an offer. This refers to the goods or services available and the particulars pertaining thereto. Thus, a meal contract has a particular start and end date. It states which meals, and how many of each, are available at a given price. It may also stipulate a dining hall to be used, a means for termination, and the institution's right to make changes and other specifics. The student then has the option of accepting or rejecting the proposed offer.

The Offer

An offer must be specific and essentially complete for it to be a valid offer. Major terms left undefined mean that there is no real offer, only an "invitation to deal." The latter is the situation one finds in many newspaper and television ads. They are not full and complete offers but only invitations to come in, see the goods, and discuss them with an offer possibly forthcoming. In *Lefkowitz* (1957), the court reviewed different newspaper ads. Many were held to be invitations, but one which was very specific, was held to be an offer. An offer must also be open for it to be accepted. If a stated time limit has run out, the offer has normally been withdrawn. An offer that is rejected is also terminated. An offer *withdrawn* by the person making it, is terminated. The offer need not be formally withdrawn however. Merely having notice from a third and trustworthy source that the offer has been withdrawn is sufficient information (*Dickinson*, 1876). In short, there are many ways to end an offer, and once that has been done, it can not be accepted by another party. The offer must be in existence for it to be accepted.

When a specific space is offered to a student for a given rent, it is an offer. If the student is also informed that that space will be held available only for three days, a time limit is set on that offer. A student desiring to claim the room on the fourth day, has no legal claim against the room, because the offer has been terminated. You may choose to give the student additional time, but that is purely up to you, you are not legally bound to do so.

You may also choose to terminate the offer before the three days are up. This can be done by contacting the student and informing him that the offer is no longer available. While this may be an unpopular act, it is a totally legal one as long as no option has been created. A good example of options can be found in *Ryder* (1976), in which the option held, even though the owner of the option changed his mind twice during its term. In *Ryder*, the plaintiff purchased an option on some land. Before the option ended he told defendant that he would not need the land involved. Defendant made other plans for the land but before the option term had ended, plaintiff again changed his mind, this time to *exercise* the option. The court holds for the plaintiff on the grounds that the defendants *must* honor his option contract. Remember that an offer must be outstanding for it to be accepted.

The Acceptance

The other side of the offer coin is that of acceptance. The party to whom the offer is extended has the power to accept. No one else can accept unless the party making the offer agrees. The accepting party actually has three courses of action available.

First, they can reject. A rejection terminates the offer. Should this party change their mind at a later date, there is no offer outstanding unless the party making the offer wishes to do so again. Thus, a rejection is an end to the process. No response at all can also be considered a rejection after a reasonable time has passed.

Second, the accepting party can counter-offer. This also terminates the original offer. It replaces it with another offer that in its turn can be either accepted or rejected. In general, there are few counter-offers in housing. Rates are set, as are the spaces available. Thus, there is little to haggle over.

Finally, the offer can be accepted. A good example of offer and acceptance forming a contract comes from the Merchant Marine Academy in *Krawez* (1969). Here, an officer of the school verbally promised immunity to students if they would testify against other students in a disciplinary hearing. They did so and the institution then tried to bring proceedings against them. The court ruled that the students were immune from discipline due to a contractual agreement. For an acceptance to be valid it must be made while the offer is still outstanding, as was recently reaffirmed by the courts of Utah where it was pointed out that rejection, conditional acceptance, or a counter-offer, all terminate the offer (*Burton*, 1976). Acceptance must also be unequivocable and *in the terms of the offer.* Anything else is not an acceptance but rather a counter-offer.

The party making the offer sets the terms and can also set the conditions of acceptance (*University Realty*, 1973). These conditions could include time, place, method of acceptance, and whether or not it needs to be in writing. Thus, you may stipulate that a student wishing to accept an offer of housing must do so no later than 3:30 P.M. on April 23rd, in the University Housing Office, and that a housing lease or license must be signed at that time. If those conditions are not met, an acceptance has not occured and you are not legally obligated to provide housing.

This may seem to be exceptionally picky, but it really is not. What it does do is give you, the offeror, the right to stay in control. You can be flexible and extend deadlines, should you care to, but at the same time, specific details permit you to terminate an offer and move on, offering the same space to other students. Indefinite details, such as "as soon as possible," or "within a reasonable time," are open to interpretation and your desired meaning simply may not be assigned. Thus, you should be as specific and detailed as possible.

One other comment should be made about acceptances. It will occasionally happen that a student will occupy an apartment or space without signing a contract for it. The student lives there for a month and then, when everyone else has been housed, he leaves saying he never signed for the unit and hence has no contract. This leaves the housing office with an unanticipated vacancy and a decrease in revenue.

The problem with the above situation is one of offer and acceptance. If no offer was outstanding, the student is a trespasser and there is no contractual claim against him, although there may be other claims. If an offer was outstanding, then occupying the space may well be an acceptance, and the contract is binding. The *offeror* always has the right to alter the acceptance methodology. Many courts would say that occupying the apartment is equal to accepting the offer and, even though no contract was formally signed, both parties agreed and hence an offer and acceptance occurred. The question here is one of intent. Was it the intent of the student to occupy the space and live there? If so, there is a contract. There can even be a contract when your communications reject the idea but your actions at that time are saying *yes* (*Crouch*, 1967).

Bargained-for Exchange and Meeting of the Minds

The philosphy of offer and acceptance, presupposes the last two pieces needed to build the consideration picture, namely "bargained-for exchange" and "a meeting of the minds." The idea behind a contract, pictures two parties of equal stature bargaining back and forth until an agreement is reached. Some contracts are indeed still negotiated that way. In general, however, contracts today are take-it-or-leave-it documents. We don't really meet individually with every student and negotiate the cost of each housing unit. Rather, a rent is set, and the student chooses to sign or not.

This is called a contract of adhesion. Basically, it is a non-bargained agreement which can be very one-sided. Because of its one-sided potential, the courts may review such an agreement more closely, looking for terms that are truly unconscionable. They do, however, uphold them and impute to them the bargained-for exchange.

All of this, the promises, the bargaining or discussion, the offer and acceptance are aimed at defining an agreement. More than that, they are aimed at defining an agreement wherein both parties have the same understanding as to what is to be done, This is the meeting of the minds. In other words, both contracting parties not only agree on the words that are to go into the contract, but they both share the same understanding as to the meaning of those words. That is a neat but important distinction. Should that not occur, both parties then would turn to the courts and ask for an interpretation favoring their side.

The court will indeed decide what the words mean. The court will look to see what was said and if any special meanings were agreed upon. If there were none, it will then turn to "industry" standards and see what the words usually mean. Should that prove fruitless, the court may well then apply the plain meaning of the words as interpreted by the hypothetical reasonable person, as was done in *Severson* (1977). To avoid all of this, you must make sure that your contractual wording is clear and unambiguous as well as being detailed. Avoid general words such as: "prompt," "modern," "soon," "reasonable." Say what you mean and then no questions of interpretation can arise. That also means that there is indeed a true meeting of the minds and hence a contract

Consideration

All of the above being present, also means that you have consideration. That term is a shorthand reference to everything being present for a contract to exist. You must have consideration if you are to have a contract. In *Godchaux Sugars, Inc.* (1940), the defendant was released from a signed agreement because there was no consideration to support it. On the other hand, consideration can merely be the abstaining from a legal act such as drinking, smoking, etc. (See *Hamer*, 1891). A shorthand means of analysis to see if consideration is present, is to do a benefit/detriment analysis.

This analysis comes from the thought that for a bargained-for exchange, an exchange of promise, an offer and acceptance, and a meeting of the minds to be present, both parties must normally gain and lose something. Thus, when you buy a car you gain the car and lose money. The seller loses the car and gains the money. The same analysis applies to student housing contracts. The student receives a benefit in the form of housing and suffers a detriment in the form of rent payments. The university receives a benefit in the form of income and, as someone once pointed out, a detriment in the form of a student. Nonetheless, the benefit/detriment analysis holds. There is consideration and hence a contract. This analysis is not very elegant but it can serve as a quick shorthand.

Now that you know that consideration must be present for a contract to exist, you should also know that there is an exception. The law has hard and firm rules with exceptions. It is this "flexibility" that allows it both to maintain its static structure and change it at the same time.

PROMISSORY ESTOPPEL

The exception is called promissory estoppel (*E.A. Coronis Associates*, 1966) This is a doctrine which comes from equity and can be used to create a contract only if consideration is not present. It is found in the concept that someone who makes a promise to another party should be forced to keep that promise, if doing otherwise would result in an injustice. Thus, if you promise someone a job and that party quits their old job to work with you, you may well be forced to employ that person even though there is no real employment contract, and you never really intended to do so (*Hoffman*, 1965). For the doctrine of promissory estoppel to apply, five elements need to be present.

First, no consideration can exist. If consideration is present, there is no need for this new doctrine because the problem can be solved by traditional contract law. Thus, the courts will apply traditional law if they can.

Second, a promise must be made—a promise which induces a second party to make a substantial life change. There are two questions of fact here: was a promise made; and was any change induced by the promise, substantial. The court would review both, and both must be present. A minor change is not adequate to support a finding of promissory estoppel.

Third, when the promise is made, the person making the promise must expect that the other party will actually rely upon the promise and make a life change. The court will go even further than this and apply a reasonable person standard in assessing reliance. That means that given the words that were used as the promise, would a reasonable person have expected the second party to rely upon them?

Fourth, the promise itself must have been the sole motivating factor for the second party's actions. If the second party would have acted in this manner even if the promise was not made or because some other promise was made, then the original promise was not the cause of the change. For promissory estoppel to apply, there must be a closed loop of self-contained cause and effect. The actions that occur must be brought about by the promise, and by it alone. They must be significant and involve some loss if the promise is not fulfilled. They must also be actions that a reasonable person would envision occurring once the promise is made. Thus, you must have a promise, a foreseeable action, the action occurring based on reliance and ultimately, a substantial change, for this doctrine to be applied.

Finally, the court will apply promissory estoppel if it is the *only* way to avoid injustice. If the problem has other solutions, they are preferred. If the problem does not have any other solutions, then the court will step in and apply its own solutions.

Basically, the court has two options. It can apply the typically legal solution of damages. In this situation, it is the desire of the court to make the injured party whole again. This goal can be achieved by computing the costs and awarding the sum to the injured party. This type of settlement is direct and immediate. It has the virtue of a definite sum and often a one-time payment. The other possible settlement comes from equity and is based upon the idea that money is an insufficient answer. Here the court would direct "specific performance" or the actual fulfillment of the promise. For this settlement to be employed, the object of the promise would need to be special or unique, such as an antique or land. It could also be used to claim especially desirable housing or a unique job opportunity.

To clarify all of this, consider the following example: A student living off-campus, comes to you and applies for a particular and highly desirable housing unit. As time passes, the student receives no response and goes in to discuss the situation with the Director of Housing. The director, confronted by an agitated and unreasonable student, wishes to restore order and says, "Don't worry, you will be housed." The student then rushes out, breaks his old lease, buys new furniture and prepares to move into university housing. Two days later, the student receives a form letter saying that his specific request has not been granted, but that alternative housing is available. Was there a contract? Was it breached? Clearly, there is no consideration for the director's statement. It was a promise but the question is, what did it promise? From the student's perspective, he has been promised housing, but, since he only requested a specific space, he may well feel that he has been granted that space.

The director, on the other hand, probably believes that only a general promise of housing somewhere has been made. This is the pitfall of lack of knowledge and general statements.

The court will look at this and apply a reasonable person standard. The director is a housing expert and hence held to a higher standard of care in his comment, than the student. Consequently, it is altogether possible that the court could find that the director should have expected reliance on his statements and that the student was correct in his specific understanding.

Once that hurdle is cleared, the other aspects of promissory estoppel fall neatly into line. There was substantial change in that the student cancelled his old lease and bought new furniture. He did that solely because of his reliance upon the director's promise. To allow the status quo to stand, would be to allow an injustice to be done, and contracts offer no ready solution. Thus, promissory estoppel would be applied.

The ultimate outcome may depend on whether money damages were sufficient. If equal alternative housing is available, on or off campus, then damages would probably suffice. If only lesser accommodations were available, then specific performance may well be called for, even though it would be highly disruptive. This would depend on how unique or desirable the requested housing actually is.

This example should be reviewed for its general application. Almost any type of promise could fit into the scenario. Hence, it makes sense to deal in facts and very clear communication as much as possible.

Now that the legal philosophy of contracts has been reviewed, it makes sense to turn to the actual drafting of a contract form. It may be useful for you to see what a typical lease is like in your community. Often a good stationery or office supply store can furnish one. This is not to say you should use such a form. It frequently does not apply to university needs, but it makes an interesting reference source.

PAROL EVIDENCE RULE

Any contract or occupancy agreement that you use should meet your particular and specific needs. Keep in mind that the signed agreement is going to be what is turned to, should a disagreement arise. Any term not in the contract probably will not be upheld, regardless of what conversations you may have had. This is known as the Parol Evidence Rule (*Gianni*, 1924).

This rule states that the written document is presumed to cover all the bargained-for terms. No additional oral agreements are valid unless they are supported by additional separate consideration. Thus, you should make sure that your occupancy agreement covers every area of concern that you have.

THINGS TO CONSIDER IN HOUSING AGREEMENTS

Many schools use three separate documents to achieve this end. The first is the occupancy agreement itself. It is a multi-copy document which establishes the specifics involved. It represents the actual meeting of the minds and the agreement of both sides to be bound. It identifies both parties to the agreement and the specific space to be rented. *Space* is preferred to *room*, as that gives you the opportunity to move students from space to space without concern as to any right existing for a particular room. It also establishes the rent, the frequency of payment and where payments should be made. The date of occupancy and the term of the agreement are also specified. This form is then signed by both parties and dated.

College housing may be deemed a necessity in some states, but it is always useful to have the parent or guardian sign the contract for students who are minors. This can also be achieved by the parents signing an agreement, upon admission, that the parents will be responsible for all costs incurred by the student while at school.

Normally, the institution has specific housing rules and other general rules that apply to any rented unit. These are contained in two other documents which become part of the agreement by referring to them in the occupancy agreement and stating that they apply. This is called, *incorporation by reference* and it makes both documents a part of the agreement. All of these rules must be available to the prospective tenant before the occupancy agreement is signed. It is best to supply everyone with individual copies prior to the contract being signed. After the agreement is signed, no *major* changes should be made in these rules. Doing so may be considered a fundamental change which would require the signing of a new agreement. At the same time, a change such as the social rule revision at Vassar College, in the late 60's, is acceptable so long as it is done through established procedures. In *Jones* (1969), the College was not found to have violated its contract with a student by making a fundamental change of social rules through preset procedures. The rule changes involved extending visitation hours in the residence halls. On the other hand, the elimination of a course part-way through the year, due to budget cuts, was held to be a breach of contract (*Peretti*, 1979). This merely means that reasonable care must be taken to assure that rule reviews are completed and published prior to the time to sign the agreement each year.

Those rules which are specific to housing and which clarify typical lease terms are often called the Terms and Conditions of Occupancy. Basically, they speak to the rights and responsibilities of each party and specify how each will act towards the other. Some typical areas covered in the Terms and Conditions are as follows:

- Who is eligible for housing
- What happens when eligibility changes
- Subleasing
- Early termination
- Lease renewals
- University liability
- Entry into the unit

- Breach of agreement
- Firearms
- Pets
- Cooking
- Storage
- Lockouts
- Noise
- Parking
- Disturbances

The above list represents some of the more common terms, but there are many others of equal applicability. In general, you should consider what specific areas you want to control in housing and then include a general statement in the terms and conditions. *Do not depend upon custom, or an oral agreement, to reach this end.* Putting it in writing will save trouble in the long run.

The final document to be considered, is the general University Rule Book. This could be absorbed into a larger Residential Living Rule Book, but it should be included somehow. The reasoning behind this is simple. Making a rule violation part of the occupancy agreement, gives you the option of terminating that agreement for the violation. This could be done anyway, through a disciplinary proceeding but it is easier and less likely to be challenged if it is part of the occupancy agreement. This has been done successfully by Long Island University. In *Miller* (1976), students were removed from housing, without a disciplinary hearing, for conduct deemed "unsuitable for dormitory living." The action was upheld since it was a term and condition of the contract.

Keep in mind also, that there are unwritten terms to the agreement. These are the terms implied by state and local ordinance. All localities have rules on fire safety, sanitation, utility supply, maintenance and other areas which automatically become a part of any agreement. You must become aware of the implied aspects in your locale, because the courts will hold you to them. Normally these rules state minimum acceptable conditions, and most institutions choose to stay well above them.

Local ordinances may also speak to the minimum temperature to be maintained in a unit, the minimum square footage per occupant, the nearness and number of fire exits, the types of insecticides that can be used in dwellings and so on. These rules are not to be fought or feared. Rather, they represent a one-time investment of effort to make sure that you are in compliance, followed by a periodic review to see what changes occur. Keeping up to date with these rules can save both time and disputes in the long run.

Failing to meet these rules, or any of the written terms of the agreement, means that a breach has occurred. That means that one party or the other has failed to live up to the agreement. If the other party has met all of the obligations under the contract, then the breach has caused injury and the individual can sue to be made whole. Since it is a breach that leads to damages, the content of a breach needs to be explored.

BREACH OF CONTRACT

Most breaches fall into three general categories which refer to their severity: insignificant, minor, and major.

An insignificant breach is the kind that regularly occurs in most institutions. A piece of furniture is missing and on order, but not there when the student arrives. The air conditioner is not functioning because a part is on order. The temperature in a room drops below the legal limit, but workmen are attempting to remedy the problem. These problems occur frequently and, while they are technically a breach, the "rule of reason" approach says that no significant harm is done. These problems rarely get to court and when they do they are simply dismissed.

A minor breach is of the same nature but ultimately denies the tenant of some service or good which was part of the agreement. This breach is not so fundamental as to terminate the contract but it may well be large enough to alter it. Take the examples given above and extend them for a longer period of time, and they may become minor breaches. Failure to supply student tenants with appropriate furniture for a month or a semester is indeed a breach. The student is paying for, but not receiving, these goods. The same would apply to infestation, heating/cooling difficulties, not being able to use promised kitchens, or other problems. The court would react to most of these by either forcing particular repairs, regardless of cost, or adjusting the rental charge downwards, or both. Basically, the thrust would be to end the problem if possible and to make the tenant whole by reimbursement for the value paid for but not received.

In *Behrend* (1977), the University School of Architecture was allowed to remain unaccredited for the last two years of its existence. Students who were enrolled, expected and were promised that the school would be accredited. This was a breach of contract won by the students. Damages were assessed and were to equal the difference between the value of a degree from an accredited school of architecture as opposed to a diploma from a non-accredited school.

A major breach of course, goes even further, and it is so fundamental that it speaks to the viability of the agreement itself. A recent Louisiana case clarifies this. In *Delta School of Business, Etc.* (1981), the school had recruited students with the promise of placement help. No help was forthcoming and the court viewed this as so fundamental a breach that it invalidated the contract involved.

The normal response to a major breach is two-fold. First, the contract itself no longer exists. Second, some monetary damages will need to be paid to make the injured party whole again. One breach of this nature, would be a major change in the agreement terms made by the university without the consent of the tenants. Another would be the inability to supply legally adequate heat throughout the winter. On the tenant's side, it would be the failure to pay rent or an attempt to destroy the occupied unit. Any of these, and many others, would terminate the agreement and allow the other party to sue for damages. If you desire a normally minor breach to be treated as a major breach, you should say so in the Terms and Conditions. Thus, the discharging of a fire extinguisher or the possession of a pet normally would not be regarded as a major breach. You may, however, wish to make it so. If you do, you must make it plain to the tenant up-front by including it in the Terms and Conditions. Again, specific wording and detailed, thoughtful, prior planning are a necessity.

Finally, we should step away from the specific agreement and take a look at the implications and definitions of all that we are actually doing. Information that is sent to students in brochures and bulletins has a direct effect on what you are expected to provide. In general, the courts will permit you to engage in a degree of "puffery"—that is, inflating your campus and its services to a size larger than life. Still, these documents do play a role in the contractual process, and hence, it is instructive to review the process from top to bottom.

When a student first decides to come to a university, housing information is requested along with all other data. This information on housing is not an offer of housing. It may be one of two possibilities. It may merely be a packet of information, or it may be an offer to be considered for housing.

In either event, it is information, and it is the type of information that people use to make decisions, As such, it must be reasonably accurate. Promises that are made must be met because many courts will read them into the contract. Consequently, all brochures, pamphlets, etc., should be reviewed for accuracy before they go to press. If an offer has been made, then a contract may be in the offing.

Where the university requires a fee for housing placement (i.e.: an application fee), it is in effect offering housing placement in consideration for the fee. Once the fee is received, the process must occur. It may not be a guarantee of housing, but it is a guarantee of equal consideration along with all other applicants, or consideration under the terms you have specified. Illinois recently upheld this exact point when it came to medical school admissions (*Steinberg*, 1977).

The next step, in either case, is the assignment of the student to a space, and notification of that assignment. Again, this is an offer. In effect, it says to the student, "we the University want to offer you housing in a particular space." Again, the offer should be very specific as to how, when and where the acceptance must occur. The student then has the choice of accepting the offer by signing the agreement. Hopefully, all of the rules and regulations have been made clear before the agreement is signed and, if so, then the signing of the agreement is a formal acceptance.

In general, this is the same process that applies to all student-related contracts. The contracts may be for housing, food services, social fees, library use, or admission itself. The process remains the same, and the same analysis applies. It would probably be useful to think in these formal analytical terms for a while until it becomes second nature. The key to success does not rest in a law degree but in a careful application of common sense.

LEASE OR LICENSE

The last question that needs to be explored is the difference between a lease and a license. Many schools refer to their housing contracts as an agreement or license rather than a lease. All three are valid contracts but the difference rests in the relationship that you wish to establish. Normally, institutions do not wish to offer a property interest to their student tenants. They do not wish to establish a formal landlord/tenant relationship. A lease does this and may subject you to your state landlord/tenant laws. Unless your state laws are to the contrary, a license would not do this.

As was pointed out by the Illinois court in *Cook* (1981), ". . . a license is 'an agreement which merely entitles one party to use property subject to the management and control of the other party'" (p. 407). The court examined a residence hall contract and found the key concept to be the institutional right to move students from room to room at will. Thus, the students had no property right in a specific room.

It should also be noted here that the court went past the designation that the institution gave the contract, and looked at the terms themselves. This emphasizes what was said before. To have a license or a rule, you must implement it and follow it.

SUMMARY

Keep in mind that a contract is a tool, like a hammer or a saw. It is only as good as you make it, and works only when you use it. Legal issues and problems should not be frightening. They should be dealt with the same as physical plant problems (i.e., prevention goes a long way towards eliminating them).

Think about what you need to do and formulate your agreements accordingly. Check with house counsel, or some other legal adviser, but keep their advice in perspective. They are not housing experts. Housing is the core of your operation and should have the controlling weight in any final decision. Lawyers are advisers, and ultimately the decision as to what to do, must rest with you. Programmatic considerations may well outweigh legal considerations, and only you can make that decision. In short, don't be afraid to do your job because of legal concerns. The law is only another variable to be dealt with and should be treated as such, no more, no less.

REFERENCES

Restatement of Contracts 2nd. St. Paul: American Law Institute Publishers, 1981.

Uniform Commercial Code. Brooklyn: American Law Institute, Edward Thompson Co., 1962.

Chapter V

Torts:
Your Legal Duties
and Responsibilities

Donald R. Moore

Larry Murray

INTRODUCTION

As a housing administrator, you are cursed with obligations or blessed with opportunities (depending on how you may view it) in carrying out the daily responsibilities of managing campus residence halls. The diversity of functions in your operation—ranging from maintaining safe facilities, to spotting psychological problems of residents, to supervising group activities—requires that you possess a working knowledge of legal considerations, as well as good common-sense judgment and professional training. An understanding of the law of torts is especially relevant to housing officers in assessing legal risks and providing comprehensive training for hall directors, residence assistants, maintenance staff and custodial workers.

In developing an understanding of a treatise on torts, you would normally expect at the outset to be provided with a definition of the topic. Unfortunately, no satisfactory definition has yet been found for a tort. While learned scholars have been unable to agree upon a precise definition, there is a commonly accepted abbreviation which will serve our purpose: a tort is a *civil wrong* consisting of an *act* or *omission* (other than a breach of contract) for which the court will provide a *remedy* in the form of an action for *damages* (Prosser, 1971).

While definitions may be comforting, it is far more important for you to understand the purpose and function of the law of torts. The body of tort law is concerned with the compensation of individuals for damage to their legally recognized interests. These innumerable interests are as diverse as our society itself, and inevitably they come into conflict with one another.

Arising out of the various and ever-increasing clashes of the activities of persons living in a common society, carrying on business in competition with fellow members of that society, owning property which may in any of a thousand ways affect the persons or property of others—in short, doing all the things that constitute modern living—there must of necessity be losses, or injuries of many kinds sustained as a result of the activities of others. The purpose of the law of torts is to adjust these losses, and to afford compenstion for injuries sustained by one person as the result of the conduct of another. (Prosser, 1971, p. 6, footnote omitted)

Torts and Crimes

At this point it is important for you to understand the distinction between a *tort* and a *crime*. At the same time you need to recognize that a single act or event may be both a tort and a crime, thus giving rise to both types of legal action.

A crime is deemed an offense committed against the public or citizenry as a whole. The prosecution of such offenses is initiated by the federal, state or municipal government in an effort to protect the interests of society at large. Criminal law is *not* concerned with the compensation of the injured individual, but rather seeks to *punish* the wrongdoer through fines or incarceration in an effort to deter others from repeating such behavior. For example, two students at a residence hall party become involved in an argument and one of them is seriously injured when he is struck over the head with a bottle; the injured student may file a complaint, resulting in the criminal prosecution by the state or municipality of the other student for assault and battery.

Tort actions are initiated and maintained by an individual, i.e., the injured party or plaintiff. The injured party seeks to recover a damage award as compensation for the injury or loss suffered to person or property. If the claim for damages is successful, the award is to be paid or satisfied by the wrongdoer. The same incident described above could provide the basis for a tort action in civil court by the injured student for damages against the other student. This situation could also result in a suit against the university and its employees, such as yourself, for alleged failure to properly supervise a sponsored campus activity.

Types of Torts

The foregoing example is also useful to us in distinguishing the two types of torts: *intentional torts* and *torts of negligence.* The injured student's suit against the other student would be based on the intentional tort of assault and battery. Intentional torts consist of those acts where there is an *intent* to bring about a result which will unlawfully invade the protected interests of another. Intent is established where a reasonable person, in the position or circumstances of the wrongdoer, believes that a particular result is *substantially certain* to follow. As stated by Prosser:

the distinction between intent and negligence obviously is a matter of degree. Apparently the line has been drawn by the courts at the point where the known danger ceases to be only a foreseeable risk which a reasonable man would avoid, and becomes a substantial certainty. (p. 32, footnote omitted)

This intent need not be hostile. For instance, liability may be imposed for injuries stemming from practical jokes or horseplay. It is *not* necessary that there be an intent to inflict the injury, but only that the *act* which caused the injury was intended. In *Jones*, (1976), Wittenberg University was held liable for the action of a campus security officer who intentionally fired a warning shot which accidentally struck and killed a student who was fleeing apprehension. Intentional torts include such acts as assault, battery, false imprisonment, infliction of mental distress, and trespass.

Intentional torts are mentioned here only briefly, as our discussion for your purpose will be directed primarily at the second type of tort—that of *negligence*. Actions based upon negligence are those where the actor is *not* substantially certain of the consequences which will follow an act or omission, but rather actions where there is, or should have been, an awareness of a risk or danger. In our example, a civil suit brought by the injured student against your university and you as an employee responsible for supervising residence hall activities, would be based on alleged negligence (failure to properly perform the duty to supervise the party).

ELEMENTS OF NEGLIGENCE

In order to understand torts of negligence, you should become familiar with each of the elements which must be proven if such a claim is to succeed:

1. There must be a *duty or obligation* recognized by law for an actor to conform to a certain standard of conduct or exercise a particular standard of care for the protection of others against unreasonable risks, and
2. A *failure* on the part of the actor to conform to the appropriate standard of conduct or care, and
3. Such failure is the *proximate cause* of the resulting injury, due to the close causal connection or nexus between the conduct of the actor and the resulting injury, and
4. There is *actual loss or damage* suffered by the injured party.

Generally speaking, the first two elements are combined to form what is termed *negligence*. However, once the duty to conform to a standard of care is determined and failure to so conform established, the elements of proximate cause and actual injury to person or damage to property need to be present for recovery in law for a tort of negligence. When examining these elements more closely, you find they are indeed complex in their application.

69

Standard of Conduct or Care

The foundation of tort law rests upon the presumption that there is a *uniform standard of behavior* which must be observed in our relationships and interactions with others, and that standard is one of *reasonableness*. More specifically, the law demands that each of us act as would a *reasonable person of ordinary prudence* placed in the same situation.

The *reasonable person* concept was created by the courts in order to construct an *objective* standard of behavior, and in an effort to overcome the impossibility of establishing fixed rules which would cover an infinite variety of circumstances and situations. Much has been written about this fictitious reasonable person:

> A model of all proper qualities, with only those human shortcomings and weaknesses which the community will tolerate on the occasion, "this excellent but odious character stands like a monument in our Courts of Justice, vainly appealing to his fellow citizens to order their lives after his own example.". . . [H]e is a prudent and careful man, who is always up to standard . . . a personification of a community ideal of reasonable behavior, determined by the jury's social judgment. (Prosser, 1971, p. 150-151, footnotes omitted)

This duty to act as a reasonable person in light of the circumstances is the *customary standard of care* which the law imposes. In certain situations, however, the law may demand that a greater standard of care be observed; this is the case where there is a *special relationship* among the parties involved or where there is a specific statute creating such a duty.

Absent a special relationship or statutory duty, however, the duty to be obeyed or the standard of care to be observed is defined by the risk perceived or that which should be perceived. In other words, *risk* determines *duty*. You should be aware that negligence is *not* simply to be equated with *carelessness*, but rather consists of behavior which has been determined to involve an unreasonable danger, or risk of danger to others. The risk necessarily involves a recognizable danger based upon *actual* or *presumed* knowledge of the existing circumstances, and a reasonable belief that harm may follow. This is the concept of *foreseeability*, and it is most important in determining the duty owed, or the standard of care to be observed.

Foreseeability and Special Relationships

Foreseeability is illustrated in the California case of *Tarasoff*, (1976), which involved the failure of a university psychologist to warn a female student of a patient's confessed intention to kill her. The Supreme Court of California examined the concept of duty, stating that: "In analyzing this issue, we bear in mind that legal duties are not discoverable facts of nature, but merely conclusory expressions that, in cases of a particular type, liability should be imposed for damage done" (p. 342). The court further discussed the many considerations involved in establishing that a particular duty or standard of care is owed by one individual to another including:

> the foreseeability of harm to the plaintiff, the degree of certainty that the plaintiff suffered injury, the closeness of the connection between the defendant's conduct and the injury suffered, the moral blame attached to the defendant's conduct, the policy of preventing future harm, the extent of the burden to the defendant and consequences to the community of imposing a duty to exercise care with resulting liability for breach, and the availability, cost and prevalence of insurance for the risk involved. (p. 342, footnote omitted)

The *Tarasoff* court concluded that the most important consideration enumerated was that of foreseeability.

You can also see the interplay of these important considerations and the dominance of foreseeability in *Eddy* (1980), which involved a suit to recover for personal injuries sustained in the university gymnasium when a visiting student crashed through a glass door at one end of the gymnasium. The student was participating in an "informal" intercollegiate game of "ultimate frisbee," (which was not sponsored by the university) and acknowledged that he was aware of the presence of the glass doors during the game.

However, the court noted that the duty owed by the university as a landowner to those entering the premises is that of reasonable care under the circumstances; in other words, the university was bound to maintain its facilities in a safe condition. Recognizing the inclination of college students to engage in unusual games and activities, the court held that a jury could determine that it was foreseeable that "students might use the gymnasium for the playing of games other than those for which the basketball courts had been laid out" (p. 925). Also, the court found that a jury could properly conclude that the university reasonably should have foreseen the presence of students and their guests in the gymnasium without the express permission of university officials. Finally, the court upheld the jury verdict finding the university was under a duty to protect users of the facility from danger presented by the glass doors, and noted that the risk presented could have been obviated without imposing an undue burden upon the university.

Important here are the facts that the students were using the facility without express permission, for a purpose other than that for which it was intended, were admittedly aware of the danger presented by the glass doors, and yet the university was still held liable. You can see that the court found these factors were outweighed by the fact that the activity could have been foreseen by the university and that the injurious consequences could have been prevented without undue burden. The court mentioned replacement of the glass doors with solid doors and the use of a metal screen over the glass as examples of unburdensome alternatives which would have eliminated the hazardous condition. Further illustrations of the duty to maintain safe premises are included in *Berrey* (1980), *Freed* (1979), *Isaacson* (1975), *Martinez* (1980), *Meyer* (1978), *Poulin* (1979), *Rice* (1978), and *Shannon* (1978).

Regarding the supervision and administration of residence halls, you must not overlook the fact that this duty to maintain reasonably safe premises is imposed for the protection of *persons* and their *property*. In *New* (1980), a Northern Arizona State University student brought a suit against the Arizona Board of Regents for negligence, claiming that their agents (university employees) failed to repair a defective door lock after it had been reported. The student contended that his stereo was stolen from his residence hall room as a result. While the decision in *New* did not reach the merits of this claim, it does serve to illustrate the applicability of these concepts to property as well as to persons.

To further illustrate the scope of possible damages for which you and your institution may be found liable, assume that it was not a stereo which was stolen from the student in *New*, but rather was some important academic work (such as classroom notes or the results of an extensive experiment). In such an event, it is not inconceivable that you could be liable for the economic value of the stolen property as well as the intrinsic value to the student. Specifically, the student might recover damages for mental or emotional distress suffered as a result of this traumatic event. If this seems trivial to you, consider that the student was preparing for graduation and that the stolen property consisted of all work done in connection with an honors thesis required for graduation. Furthermore, the student had already accepted a well-paying job and was soon to be married.

In such a case the liability imposed *might* extend to the: (1) economic value of the stolen property; (2) the wages lost while attempting to reconstruct the stolen work; (3) damages sustained if the job accepted was no longer available following the delayed graduation; (4) mental and emotional distress suffered as a result of losing the stolen work and losing the job; and (5) mental and emotional distress suffered as a result of a postponement or eventual cancellation of the marriage. If this seems farfetched, you should be aware that a finding of negligence against you and your employees resulting in the consequences described in this example *could* result in the recovery of all the above losses.

While you should now be aware that foreseeability is central to any decision regarding the exercise of reasonable care, it is *not* always the decisive or controlling factor. In *Baldwin* (1981), acknowledged by the court to be a case "on the cutting edge of the tort law" (p. 821), the court stated that:

Even though a harm may be foreseeable . . . a concomitant duty to prevent the harm does not always follow. "Rather, the question is whether the risk of harm is sufficiently high and the amount of activity needed to protect against harm sufficiently low to bring the duty into existence, ..." (p. 816, citation omitted)

Baldwin involved a student plaintiff and several other students, each of whom drank heavily one evening in their residence hall. The drinking activity was in violation of the residence hall license agreement, though the student alleged that the resident assistants knowingly permitted the possession and consumption of alcoholic beverages within the residence halls. Later that evening, the student suffered injuries in an automobile accident (which resulted from a speeding contest) involving defendant drivers who had been involved in the earlier drinking activity. Subsequently, the student sued the university trustees, the university governing body, and two residence hall advisors based upon their alleged failure to enforce the drinking prohibition.

The court began its discussion by noting that the student based his complaint upon the alleged nonfeasance (an omission or failure to act) rather than misfeasance (taking action improperly) of the university and its employees. In cases of nonfeasance, a duty is recognized and resulting liability imposed only upon a showing that a *special relationship* exists between the parties involved. In this case the special relationship would need to exist "between the Trustees on the one hand, and the plaintiff and student defendants on the other" (p. 812). It is a special relationship in the sense that it would place upon the university the responsibility of preventing the injury which was sustained, though the injury was occasioned by the act of a third party. In this case, however, the court found that the housing agreement relied upon by the student, was insufficient to constitute such a special relationship.

Furthermore, in refusing to impose liability upon the university, the court in *Baldwin* looked to factors noted previously in the *Tarasoff* (1976) decision and concluded: (1) that there was "a lack of a close connection between the failure of the Trustees and dormitory advisors to control on-campus drinking and the speed contest" (p. 816); (2) that the university was not morally blameworthy for their omission; and (3) that it would impose upon the university a difficult and substantial burden if it were charged with policing its campus so as to eradicate the consumption of alcohol. However, the court noted the particular facts in this case, and distinguished it from a situation where the university administrators and employees (such as housing officials) might be involved to a greater extent, or possessed with a greater degree of knowledge. Specifically, the court noted in *Baldwin* (1981) the "lack of direct involvement [by university administrators] with the furnishing of alcoholic beverages" (p. 818).

Finally, the court examined in detail the evolution of the relationship between a university and its students. This discussion borrowed heavily from the language and opinion in *Bradshaw* (1979). *Bradshaw* involved a student who sought to recover damages from Delaware Valley College for injuries sustained in an automobile accident which followed an off-campus sophomore class picnic. The automobile in which the student was riding was being driven by another student who became intoxicated at the picnic. The sophomore class faculty advisor and members of the college administration participated in the planning and promotion of the party, and were apparently aware that free beer would be served. State law and college regulations prohibited the use of alcoholic beverages by persons under the age of twenty-one. Also, there were no representatives of the faculty nor the administration in attendance to supervise the picnic.

The *Bradshaw* court initially pointed out that "the modern American college is not an insurer of the safety of its students. Whatever may have been its responsibility in an earlier era, the authoritarian role of today's college administrations has been notably diluted in recent decades" (p. 138). Also noted was the abatement of the doctrine of *in loco parentis*, and the recognition that colleges and universities no longer have a duty to exercise such control over the conduct of a student, as would a parent. The changes in the relationship between institutions and their students are a result of student demands that they be given greater control in defining and regulating their own lives. The court found that this reapportionment of responsibilities greatly affects the field of torts: "Thus, for purposes of examining fundamental relationships that underlie tort liability, the competing interests of the student and the institution of higher learning are much different today than they were in the past" (p. 140).

As in *Baldwin* (1981), the student in the *Bradshaw* case sought to establish that the college had a duty to protect him from harm caused by the acts of a third party. Again, such claims are valid only upon the establishment of some special relationship between the college and the students involved. The student argued that the regulations prohibiting the use of alcoholic beverages by students under age twenty-one created a custodial relationship between the parties, whereby a duty of protection would be imposed. However, the court was not persuaded by this argument and held that under Pennsylvania law the college had *not* "voluntarily taken custody of Bradshaw so as to deprive him of his normal power of self-protection or to subject him to association with persons likely to cause him harm" (p. 141).

In a related argument, the court in *Bradshaw* (1979) further held that no special relationship was created by the fact that the college had knowledge that beer would be available at the picnic. While the student alleged that the college had both the opportunity and capability to control beer drinking at an off-campus function, and a concomitant duty to do so, the court disagreed: "Under these circumstances, we think it would be placing an impossible burden on the college to impose a duty in this case" (p. 142).

In both *Bradshaw* and *Baldwin* the courts failed to find that a special relationship existed between the injured party and the university or college. Thus, the courts failed to charge the educational institutions with the duty of protecting their students from the harmful acts of third parties. In both cases, the educational institutions were possessed of some degree of knowledge regarding the potential for harmful conduct. However, the courts looked to many of the other factors previously mentioned (such as the burden to the defendant, social policy implications, closeness of the connection between the conduct of the defendant and the injury, etc.) in concluding that a duty should not be imposed.

However, you should be keenly aware that there are circumstances in which the courts have recognized the *existence* of a special relationship between an institution of higher education and its students. In *Duarte* (1979), a parent brought a suit against the State, seeking damages for the wrongful death of her daughter. The daughter, a freshmen student at California State University (at San Diego), was raped and murdered in her residence hall room by a Navy seaman. Again, since this case is one in which the harmful conduct was directly due to the act of a third party, the university will be liable only upon the showing of a special relationship. As in *Baldwin* (1981) and *Bradshaw* (1979), the most important factors to be examined are: (1) the *relationship* among the parties involved; and (2) the extent to which the university was aware, or should have been aware, of the dangers presented, i.e., *foreseeability*.

In looking at the relationship factor, the *Duarte* court quoted from the landmark landlord-tenant decision in *Kline* (1970) and said:

The landlord is no insurer of his tenants' safety, but he is certainly no bystander . . . [S]ince the ability of one of the parties to provide for his own protection has been limited in some way by his submission to the control of the other, a duty should be imposed upon the one possessing control (and thus the power to act) to take reasonable precautions to protect the other one from assaults by third parties which, at least, could reasonably have been anticipated. (p. 724)

The *Duarte* court held that the female student, through her housing agreement with the university, had surrendered some control of her own security. Specifically, she was prohibited from employing various means of self-protection such as the installation of security measures or the possession of a watchdog or firearm. The court found that the victim had a "landlord-tenant relationship-plus" (p. 735) with the university, thus constituting a duty-imposing special relationship.

Following the recognition of a duty owed by the university to the student victim, the court looked to the now familiar question of knowledge or foreseeability; for while the relationship establishes the duty, the question of knowledge or foreseeability determines whether there has been a breach of that duty so as to impose liability. According to the mother of the victim, the university was aware that many nonstudents were attracted to the campus in hopes of establishing relationships with the young women on campus. Furthermore, it was alleged that the university was aware of a chronic pattern of escalating assaults, rapes, and attacks upon its young female students, and that there was in fact a cover-up of this information by the university.

Unfortunately, the decision in the case does not resolve this question of foreseeability. The court merely held that the mother of the victim had sufficiently stated a legal claim for which relief *could* be granted. There was no determination of liability at this stage; the court simply made it clear that the establishment of the special relationship, as outlined above, and proof of the allegations of knowledge by the university, would result in the imposition of liability upon the university.

In reviewing the *Tarasoff* (1976), *Baldwin* (1981), *Bradshaw* (1979), and *Duarte* (1979) cases, it should be apparent to you that the imposition of liability upon the university, for damages occurring as the result of third-party acts, is predicated upon the establishment of a special relationship between the university and the injured party. Also, it is clear that just as in other cases which do not involve special relationships, foreseeability is a critical factor in determining whether there has been a breach of the established duty. These cases point out that liability is most likely to be imposed when you, as the agent or employee of the institution, have notice of probable or impending harm and you fail to take reasonable steps to ensure the safety of your students. Other cases involving special relationships include *Jesik* (1980), *McIntosh* (1979), *Schultz* (1975), *University of Alaska* (1976), and *Villalobos* (1980).

Proximate Cause

After a determination of a breach of a recognized duty (negligence), a further causal connection between such negligence and the resulting injury is necessary for the imposition of liability. This element is referred to as *proximate cause*. There is "perhaps nothing in the entire field of law which has called forth more disagreement, or upon which the opinions are in such a welter of confusion" (Prosser, p. 236).

At first glance, you may conclude that the concept of proximate cause seems simple: the negligent party is responsible for the injurious consequences flowing from such conduct. Philosophically, however, the consequences of any particular act carry forward to eternity. Thus, at some point a line must be drawn beyond which the consequences will be deemed too remote to demand the imposition of liability. Recalling the hypothetical example of the student whose honors thesis work was stolen from the residence hall room—do you think that the failure of the university employees to promptly repair the defective lock was the proximate cause of the student's cancelled marriage? According to Prosser:

> As a practical matter, legal responsibility must be limited to those causes which are so closely connected with the result and of such significance that the law is justified in imposing liability. Some boundary must be set to liability for the consequences of any act, upon the basis of some social idea of justice or policy. (p. 236-237)

In an attempt to establish such a boundary, courts have generally accepted that the negligence of the wrongdoer is the cause of the event when it is a *material element* and a *substantial factor* in bringing about the event. While such a standard may seem ambiguous, it does signal an attempt to somehow limit the imposition of liability.

This is illustrated in *Hall* (1981), where a female student was shot in the lobby of her residence hall. The assailant had been sitting quietly in the waiting area of the residence hall when suddenly, without warning or provocation, he pulled a revolver and shot the student as she awaited an elevator. The student sought to recover damages from the university based upon the alleged inadequacy of the campus security force.

Though there was evidence of prior isolated incidents of violence on campus, the court concluded that the "failure to implement a given level of security protection is not a proximate cause of a particular act where the event might have occurred in spite of utmost security precautions" (p. 1126). The court recognized that even the most sophisticated security force would be unable to protect students from a spontaneous, unprovoked act of violence, and thus refused to extend the scope of proximate cause so as to include such consequences.

However, in order to appreciate the subjectivity of this standard, you should contrast the decision in *Hall* with that in *Meese* (1981). In *Meese*, a student registered for a beginners' ski class, and rented all the necessary equipment from the university bookstore. The skis were rented to the student by a part-time employee, who briefly examined and adjusted the tension on the ski bindings. During the second day of instruction on the slopes, the student was injured while attempting a "snowplow turn." The injury required surgery and the student sought damages for the negligence of the bookstore employee, due to his failure to properly adjust the ski bindings.

The university argued that the damage to the student's knee was not the result of improperly adjusted bindings, and that the fall would have caused such an injury even if the bindings had been properly adjusted. The university attempted to show that this *superseded* their negligence, and was the proximate cause of the injury.

While recognizing that the "forces that are brought into play on a ski slope that result in an injury to a skier are difficult to define" (p. 723), the court rejected the superseding cause argument and concluded that the negligence of the bookstore employee was the proximate cause. In other words, while the direct cause of the injury may have been the fall itself, the court determined the proximate cause to be the negligence of the bookstore employee.

What is important for you to realize, is that *proximate cause* is not to be equated with *cause in fact*. At times the law may limit the scope of consequences for which an act will be deemed the proximate cause, while at other times the law seems to reach out in order to establish that a particular act or omission is the proximate cause of the harmful consequence. The concept of proximate cause serves as a repository for considerations of social policy which may affect the imposition of liability.

NEGLIGENCE DEFENSES

Even when the plaintiff or injured party has proven negligence, the defendant may be excused from liability if it can be proven that the plaintiff: (1) contributed to the injury or damage through fault or negligence; or (2) assumed the risk which caused the injury or damage. These defenses are referred to as *contributory negligence* and *assumption of risk*, respectively. In examining each of these concepts more closely, you should keep in mind that these are referred to as *affirmative defenses* in the great majority of jurisdictions. Affirmative defenses require that the defendant bear the burden of proof. For example, a speeding driver may be negligent in striking a student who is crossing a campus intersection. However, the driver may avoid or limit liability for the accident if it can be shown that the student was at fault in crossing the street against a traffic signal.

Contributory Negligence

The concept of contributory negligence is founded upon a policy which demands that individuals use due care and prudence to protect their own legally recognized interests. Contributory negligence may be defined as "conduct on the part of the plaintiff, contributing as a legal cause to the harm he has suffered, which falls below the standard to which he is required to conform for his own protection" (Prosser, p. 416-417, footnote omitted). The standard of conduct is the same as in the case of ordinary negligence—that of a *reasonable person* of *ordinary prudence* under similar circumstances.

As in the case of ordinary negligence, *causation* is an element which must be satisfied as it relates to contributory negligence. There exists in the courts some confusion with respect to causation. Some courts have held that this element is satisfied when the injured party has contributed to the injury "in any degree, however slight" (Prosser, p. 421). Other courts have reasoned that the conduct must be a *material element* and a *substantial factor* in causing the injury.

Once the elements of negligence and proximate cause are established, the defendant may introduce the defense of contributory negligence. Furthermore, the scope of the defense may be far-reaching. In a jurisdiction governed by the policy of *strict contributory negligence*, the establishment of such negligence constitutes a *complete bar* to recovery by the plaintiff. Thus, if an individual deviates only slightly from the established standard of conduct, this doctrine provides that compensation *cannot* be awarded for the damage or loss suffered. For example, in a case involving an automobile accident between two cars, a jury may determine that both parties were at fault to some degree. The jury may find the degree of negligence attributable to one party to be much greater than that of the other; regardless, if the plaintiff is found to be only 10% at fault, there would be *no* recovery for damages from the defendant who was 90% at fault.

For this reason, several alternatives have appeared which serve to eliminate this seemingly harsh result. In some jurisdictions, the existence of contributory negligence on the part of the plaintiff acts as a total bar to recovery *only* when it reaches a prescribed level. These are referred to as systems of *modified comparative negligence*, of which there are three variations: (1) *equal to or greater than*; (2) *not greater than*; and (3) *slight-gross rule.*

Under the equal to or greater than rule, the plaintiff is barred from recovery where the degree of negligence (contributory) attributable to the plaintiff, is greater than or equal to that of the defendant.[1] In contrast, the *not greater than* system provides that the plaintiff may recover diminished damages (reduced in proportion to the plaintiff's contributory negligence) only if plaintiff's negligence was not greater than that of the defendant.[2] The crucial difference between the two is shown when fault is equally divided; under the first variation the plaintiff can recover nothing, but is entitled to recover 50% of damages under the second variation. On the other hand, the *slight-gross rule* bars recovery unless the plaintiff's negligence is slight and the defendant's gross, in comparison.[3] Collectively, these systems of modified comparative negligence are the most widely accepted methods of apportioning fault. Another approach taken, is that of a jury strictly apportioning liability among the parties based upon a determination of

---

[1]Applied in the following states: Arkansas, Colorado, Georgia, Idaho, Kansas, Maine, North Dakota, Utah, West Virginia, and Wyoming. Note, *Comparative Negligence*, 81 Colum. L.Rev. 1668, 1672, n.28 (1981).

[2]Applied in the following states: Connecticut, Hawaii, Massachusetts, Minnesota, Montana, Nevada, New Hampshire, New Jersey, Oklahoma, Oregon, Pennsylvania, Texas, Vermont, and Wisconsin. *Id.* at 1673, n.30.

[3]Applied in Nebraska and South Dakota. *Id.* at 1674, n.36.

the comparative degrees of fault or negligence—commonly referred to as *pure comparative negligence*[4].

Comparative Negligence

Again, these concepts of comparative negligence are the most recent alternatives advanced in response to the policy of strict contributory negligence, and not a new element in and of itself. Under this system, each party found to be negligent in some degree (whether it be ordinary or contributory in nature) is likewise liable to that same extent for the resulting injury.

For example, the student who was injured while skiing in *Meese* (1981) was also found to be contributorily negligent. Specifically, the court found that the student was inattentive in class at a time when instructions were being given as to how to properly check the ski bindings. This was found to have constituted 25% of the negligence, and under the doctrine of comparative negligence the university was held liable for only 75% of the student's injury. These comparative percentages of negligence are questions which are determined by the jury.

Zavala (1981) is another example where the doctrine of contributory negligence is applied in a system governed by comparative negligence. In *Zavala*, a twenty-three year old nonstudent attended a residence hall party at the Santa Cruz campus of the University of California. Before arriving at the party, he had consumed several beers and smoked two-thirds of a pipe of marijuana. At the residence hall party sponsored by the resident assistants and the hall preceptors, the plaintiff drank six cups of beer from the first keg and an unknown number of cups from the second keg. He also drank three-quarters of a pint of apricot brandy that he brought along. Subsequently, he and several friends retired to the friend's residence hall room. A few minutes later the plaintiff asked his friends for directions to the bathroom, and upon leaving the room proceeded to a balcony located between the third and fourth floors of the hall. Amazingly, the 5'4" plaintiff managed to fall over a 3'7" stairwell balcony wall.

In the plaintiff's suit, the trial court found the university negligent because alcoholic beverages were served to an obviously intoxicated person. However, the trial court also found the plaintiff to be contributorily negligent, holding that the prior consumption of alcohol and smoking of marijuana constituted willful misconduct. Thus, the jury apportioned 80% of the negligence to the plaintiff and 20% to the university.

Last Clear Chance

The concept of "last clear chance" also owes its origin to what many felt were the harsh results produced by the doctrine of strict contributory negligence, and was once the most commonly accepted

---

[4]Applied in the following states: Alaska, California, Florida, Illinois, Louisiana, Michigan, Mississippi, New York, Rhode Island, and Washington. *Id.* at 1671, n.18.

modification of that doctrine. A statement of this legal concept is: "[I]f the defendent has the clear opportunity to avoid the harm, the plaintiff's negligence is not a 'proximate cause' of the result" (Prosser, p. 427). Thus, the plaintiff's contributory negligence may be completely excused if the defendant is found to have had the *last clear chance* to avoid the injury. You should realize that the plaintiff must prove the following elements in order to establish that the last clear chance rested with the defendant: (1) the defendant was *aware* or *should have been aware*, of the situation; (2) the defendant had an *opportunity* to take the necessary action to *avoid* the harm; and (3) the defendant *failed* to do that which a *reasonable person* would have done.

While the burden of proving last clear chance seems substantial, many legal writers feel the doctrine still produces some undesirable results. In practice, the greater the negligence of the defendant, the less the liability may be. As Prosser states: "The driver who looks carefully and discovers the danger, and is then slow in applying his brakes, may be liable, while the one who does not look at all . . . may not" (p. 433). However, as the number of states adopting some form of comparative negligence continues to grow, the doctrine of last clear chance will likely continue to fade; the contemporary view appears to be that the concept of comparative negligence supersedes and eliminates the need for the doctrine of last clear chance.

Assumption of Risk

There are two variations on the theme of assumption of risk: express and implied. *Express assumption of risk* occurs when the plaintiff expressly consents in advance to relieve the defendant of the obligation to observe a particular standard of care or where the plaintiff enters into a relationship with the defendant with knowledge that the defendant will not provide protection against a particular risk. *Implied assumption of risk* exists where the plaintiff is aware of some danger already created by the negligence of the defendant, but nevertheless voluntarily proceeds to encounter it.

The doctrine of assumption of risk is also akin to contributory negligence. While many view assumption of risk as the elimination of the duty owed to the plaintiff by the defendant, others see it as a form of contributory negligence where the negligence consists of making the wrong choice, that is, voluntarily encountering a known unreasonable risk. As a result, the two doctrines are often confused and rarely are distinguished clearly. Suffice it to say, "[t]he significant difference, when there is one, is likely to be one between risks which were in fact known to the plaintiff, and risks which he merely might have discovered by the exercise of ordinary care" (Prosser, p. 441, footnotes omitted).

The most common example of express assumption of risk which would be of particular interest to housing officers, occurs through the use of *release forms*. In *Doyle* (1979), a private college sponsored a two-week hockey clinic at which one of the participants was injured. The injury occurred when a plastic hockey blade flew off the end of a hockey stick and partially blinded the plaintiff's son. In the resulting tort suit, the jury awarded damages in the amount of $50,000.

The college appealed this award, contending that documents signed by the parents prior to their son's participation in the clinic excused the institution from liability. The release form signed by the injured boy's mother read as follows:

> I fully understand that Bowdoin College, its employees or servants will accept no responsibility for or on account of any injury or damage sustained by Brian arising out of the activities of the said THE CLINIC. I do, therefore, agree to assume all risk of injury or damage to the person or property of Brian arising out of the activities of the said THE CLINIC. (p. 1207)

In refusing to overturn the lower court's imposition of liability upon the college, the Supreme Judicial Court of Maine characterized the general view the judiciary has for such agreements:

> Courts have traditionally disfavored contractual exclusions of negligence liability and have exercised a heightened degree of judicial scrutiny when interpreting contractual language which allegedly exempts a party from liability for his own negligence. (p. 1207)

The court found that the language of the release agreement failed to specifically spell out the intention of the parties to contractually extinguish negligence liability. The court noted that ambiguous language in such an agreement must be construed against the party seeking to enforce the agreement and thereby escape liability. The *Doyle* court found that the agreement merely indicated an "unwillingness" by the college to shoulder any additional burden that it would not bear otherwise, and upheld the $50,000 damage award. *Gross* (1978) provides an additional example of liability in a situation involving a release form.

With regard to establishing an implied assumption of risk, you should be aware of two important requirements: (1) the plaintiff must be *aware of* and must *fully comprehend* the risk incurred; and (2) the decision to incur such risk must be given *voluntarily* and *freely*. The major importance of these requirements is the apparent replacement of our *reasonable person of ordinary prudence* standard (used throughout the area of tort law) with a more subjective standard keyed to the particular plaintiff. In practice, however, the standard applied does not differ greatly from that of the *reasonable person*.

In *Scaduto* (1982), a student was injured while participating in an intramural softball game held on a college campus field. The injury occurred when the student stepped into the indentation of a drainage ditch while attempting to catch a ball in foul territory. The student maintained that the ditch constituted an inherently hazardous condition and that the college had violated its duty of reasonable care owed to those participating in the game.

Reversing the decision of the lower court, the appellate court held that the student had voluntarily elected to participate in the game, and had thus "assumed the dangers of the game. This included the possibility of falling while in pursuit of the ball" (p. 530). Also important was the fact that the drainage ditch was clearly visible to the players and that the plaintiff was aware of its location. Based upon these findings, the appellate court held that the college did not breach its duty of care and was not liable for the plaintiff's injuries.

This doctrine of implied assumption of risk has been criticized by many who see it as barring recovery in cases of genuine hardship—much like the strict rule of contributory negligence. Consequently, assumption of risk is currently recognized on a more limited basis than ever before, although it is not likely to disappear anytime soon.

VICARIOUS LIABILITY

Vicarious liability, or imputed negligence, is a concept through which *A* is *responsible* and *liable* for the tortious conduct of *B*, as a result of the *relationship* between *A* and *B*, even though *A* has done *nothing* whatsoever *to aid* or *encourage* the tortious conduct of *B*. The most familiar example of this doctrine is the liability imposed upon the master, for torts committed by servants; in contemporary terms, we refer to the parties as *employer* and *employee*. The application of this broad doctrine to the particular relationship between employer and employee, is referred to as *respondeat superior* or "look to the man higher up." Under the concept of *respondeat superior*, an employer (your university, or you as a supervisor) is responsible for the tortious conduct of employees (you or one of your staff members) so long as the employees are acting *within the course or scope of their employment*. An act within the course or scope of employment is somewhat vague, but generally the phrase:

refers to those acts which are so closely connected with what the servant is employed to do, and so fairly and reasonably incidental to it, that they may be regarded as methods, even though quite improper ones, of carrying out the objectives of the employment. (Prosser, p. 460)

Courts and juries examine many factors in order to establish whether the conduct is *closely connected* and *reasonably incidental* to the employment. These factors include the *time*, *place*, and *purpose* of the act, the *degree* to which it *deviates* from what is authorized, the *extent* to which such conduct could have been *foreseen* by the employer, and many others. Another factor to be considered is whether or not the employee's act was *forbidden* by the employer.

Though this factor is not strictly determinative, it is an important consideration. However, you should also know that if the tortious conduct is merely the employee's method of getting the job done, it is unlikely that the employer will escape liability because the method used was prohibited.

The concept of *respondeat superior* has even been expanded to the field of intentional torts. In general, the employer is liable for the intentional torts of employees where the purpose—however misguided—is to some degree in furtherance of the employer's business interest. Clearly, you (and through you, the university) *may* be liable for the actions of your residence hall assistants should they become involved in a scuffle while attempting to enforce hall rules and regulations; restrain someone in an attempt to restore order during a disturbance; allow one student access to the room of another, or endless other examples.

With respect to your employment of an off-campus independent contractor to perform work in the residence halls, the general rule is that the institution is not vicariously liable for torts committed by the contractor. This is based on the premise that the manner in which the work is performed and the supervision of workers on the job are under the control of the independent contractor. However, you should be aware that you have a duty to carefully select a qualified independent contractor to avoid possible liability.

GOVERNMENTAL IMMUNITY

While you may find vicarious liability a bit intimidating, some protection in the form of an immunity may be afforded state schools and their employees. Public educational institutions (and their officers and administrators) are generally considered to be instrumentalities or agencies of the state, and as such may be protected from tort liability by the doctrine of *governmental* or *sovereign immunity*. This doctrine originated during the earlier days of the divine rights of kings, and provided that the sovereign or state could not be sued without its consent. Specifically, an officer of the state could not be sued in an official capacity for the negligent performance of a duty. Of course, the officer could always be held liable for personal or private torts committed outside the sphere of official duties (*Holzer*, 1981; *Jagnandan*, 1976; and *Ronwin*, 1981).

Currently, the trend of state governments is moving in the direction of *limiting* or *eliminating* the broad doctrine of sovereign immunity. Many states have already done so, with less than a dozen still retaining full sovereign immunity. While the trend is to reduce the scope of this doctrine, many observers contend that some measure of immunity must be retained.

In states that have recently waived (to some extent) their immunity, an exception has been carved out which is based upon whether or not the act or omission giving rise to the tort was of a ministerial or a discretionary nature. *Ministerial acts* are described as those amounting to a mere obedience of orders, while *discretionary acts* are those requiring personal deliberation and the exercise of judgment. Generally, the immunity has been preserved with regard to discretionary acts (*DeStafney*, 1982; *Dizick*, 1979; *Hennessy*, 1980; and *Lister*, 1976).

In *Relyea* (1980), two female students were abducted from a Florida Atlantic University campus parking lot, and later murdered. The girls were abducted as they returned to their car, following a late afternoon class at a remote location on campus. The parents and administrators of the estates of the deceased girls filed a suit against the Florida Board of Regents, alleging that the university was negligent in failing to provide adequate security for the protection of its students. The Florida Board of Regents based their defense on a claim of sovereign immunity in the exercise of a discretionary function.

The court in *Relyea* began by recognizing that the university system and its governing board were instrumentalities of the state, and protected by the doctrine of sovereign immunity when exercising a discretionary function (according to the law of the state of Florida). Furthermore, the court pointed out that:

> the decisions of the campus security force regarding its modus operandi, i.e. where and how to deploy its available manpower, the number of security personnel per shift, the use of telecommunications equipment, and the extent of coordination with local law enforcement agencies are discretionary or planning functions. (p. 1382)

As a result, the court held that in the exercise of such discretionary functions, the Florida Board of Regents was protected by sovereign immunity. The court distinguished this from a situation where a tort might be committed during the implementation of a particular security objective—such as the accidental discharge of a firearm.

Finally, it should be noted that the majority of the state courts will uphold immunity only where the official is determined to have acted *honestly* and in *good faith*. As you would imagine, there is no immunity for acts done in a *malicious* or *improper* manner (*Wood*, 1975).

SUMMARY

While this has been a limited overview of the law of torts and its application to college housing administrators, a study of the information should increase your awareness of the potential legal risks associated with your responsibilities. A better understanding of legal consequences provides a sounder basis for decision making and avoidance of liability. It can hopefully transform an attitude of thinking that you are cursed with obligations to one of feeling blessed with opportunities.

As was mentioned at the outset, tort law is a dynamic, growing field of law. In our society, parties are increasingly turning to the courts to resolve disputes and recover damages. With respect to tort law, the question of whether or not a tort has been committed, and what (if any) damages should be awarded, is generally decided by the jury. All of the above factors combine to make an impersonal entity such as an educational institution, a likely target for the imposition of liability.

Finally, you should note that tort law is a function of state law. The legal principles and existing jurisprudence or case-law applicable to any tort situation will vary from state to state. Therefore, this brief discussion should in no way serve as a substitute for legal advice. Hopefully, you recognize more than ever the need to work closely with the legal counsel or the risk management department of your university.

REFERENCES

Grehan, K. Notes: Comparative Negligence. *Columbia Law Review.* 1981, *81*(8), 1668-1701.

Prosser, W. *Law of Torts* (4th Ed.). St. Paul, Minn.: West Publishing Co., 1971.

Chapter VI

Managing the Risk

Stephen T. Miller

A given of our complex society is that life is beset by risk. Crossing the street can be a death defying act and even breathing the air may be dangerous—yet, we do it because the alternatives may be more costly. Risk is not to be feared but rather recognized, controlled and perhaps minimized. Doing this does not remove the risk but it does manage it and that is what this section is about. Legal risks are very real in our litigious society. Many housing professionals are threatened with suit three or four times a year, but suits often do not materialize. Thus, suit is a risk, but one with which we are coping quite well. Keeping a few simple concepts in mind will greatly reduce even the current small likelihood of a legal fight. These rules are largely common sense and deserve to be viewed in that light.

CONSISTENCY

We all know that consistency is the hobgoblin of small minds. It is also one of the surest ways to avoid personal and institutional liability. We must deal with students as individuals, as consumers and as members of very conscious constituencies.

In the past, visceral responses by administrators to questions, often went unchallenged even if they conflicted with a response to another student. This often is not the case today. Little happens in a vacuum and students are very aware of what you are saying to other students. They may often be quick to interpret an answer as being prejudicial and based upon race, sex, national origin, etc., rather than rational deliberation. It is always hard to accept "no" as an answer. It becomes especially so when the student is convinced, rightly or wrongly, that the answer was motivated not by the situation but by prejudice from whatever source.

This is not to say that responses can not take into account individual needs. They can indeed. What is needed, however, is a consistent rational procedure for generating answers. A capricious response is asking for a rebuttal. If we have rules on the issue, we must apply them uniformly. If we make exceptions, we must make them uniformly and be able to explain in meaningful terms why the exception was made. In *Poynter* (1972), a district court upheld different residential requirements for students over twenty-three years of age. The court found that the college had advanced rational reasons for two different rules. However, the decision in *Cooper* (1972), went the other way. There the court found that the rules deciding housing were not as detailed, nor did they have the *rational basis* found in *Poynter*.

For example, in the first week of September, many university housing facilities are overcrowded. In some instances almost anyone who comes in and asks to go off-campus receives permission to do so. By mid-October, sufficient vacancies may have appeared to house everyone. Terminations of student contracts are now very limited or non-existent. This is not capricious or prejudicial. It reflects a real institutional need, and written policies on termination should reflect it. Thus, equal treatment of students in September and October may be entirely different but still equal within the defined groups (i.e., overcrowded housing vs. non-overcrowded). Again, having consistent responses to legitimate student requests goes a long way towards reducing risk. Arbitrary decisions are nearly always reversed, as the court did in *Levine* (1976) and *State ex. rel. Bartlett* (1971).

RULES AND ENFORCEMENT

It may seem that every year we have more and more rules. They are designed to aid us in the decision-making process and to guard us against the capricious response. It can also be comforting to say that a rule controls a situation, and there is nothing that we can do. The question is, though, is that true? In reality, we often have rules on the books that are bent, fractured and even broken. We ultimately fall back upon them only when forced. Many other times, we look the other way and prefer not to enforce a rule. This gives us two problems. One is that of capricious enforcement as discussed above. The other is whether or not the rule actually exists.

Having a rule on the books does not mean that it exists. Enforcement is needed to give it life and regular enforcement to give it vigor. Lack of enforcement is telling students that *custom*, not rule, governs in a particular situation. In turn, should a problem arise, the court will go past the rule to the actuality. This is the basis for the many court cases questioning procedures in discipline cases of both students and employers. In *Heisler* (1982), the court reinstated an academically dismissed student because set procedures were not appropriately fol-

88

lowed. It is not enough to have the procedure; we must follow it in practice, for it to exist.

Thus, if we wish to limit our tort liability by forbidding students access to the roofs of dormitories, that is acceptable. However, unless we enforce it by making sure everyone is aware of the rule, making a reasonable effort to bar entry to the roof, having a security officer remove students found on the roof, and having a disciplinary hearing with appropriate penalties we do not have a rule. Enforcement does not mean that no one will ever go on the roof. It does mean, however, that we have made a good faith effort to end roof access and, hence, meet our duty in the matter.

The same concept applies in all areas where we have rules. Not only does this concept apply to students (*Tedeschi*, 1980), but it also applies to employees and their roles, as a recent Virginia decision illustrates (*Jacobs*, 1980). It applies to all procedures, whether in discipline or in room draw. In short, it applies to all rules and regulations.

Take time to review your rules and regulations and keep them up to date. You may wish to drop those that really are not enforced. In any event, do not depend on protection from rules that do not exist because they are not enforced.

BINDING THE UNIVERSITY

A university is much like any large company in that it buys and sells goods and services. The question that arises in these interactions is just who can buy and sell for the university? Who has the authority to commit the institution to a particular answer, promise, sale, or purchase (*Anderson*, 1978)? In an Alabama case (*In re Tuskegee*, 1977) it was held that the institution was liable for goods purchased by employees who never had the authority to make the purchase. Most institutions have rules regarding this, and they are generally known among most employees. The problem often flows from their lack of specificity and the impressions that we convey to innocent third parties.

For example, a student entering the housing office may ask a question of a student employee or receptionist and get an answer which goes against policy. The student then leaves and acts in accordance with that answer. Or again, a merchant in the community is accustomed to dealing with the university. Often, the university orders goods informally and picks them up shortly thereafter. One day, a university truck drives up and an individual wearing university work clothes purchases supplies. These goods never reach the university but the bill does (*R.H. Kyle Furniture, Co.*, 1960)! Is there a binding contract?

The court may well look at these incidents and desire to protect an innocent third party acting in good faith. Consequently, the university may be bound to the promise or the contract by its employees.

In both of these cases, the third party dealt with one who had the trappings of authority (*Alterman*, 1957). In other words, in the absence of prior knowledge, a reasonable person in the same situation would think that the receptionist or the maintenance person spoke for the university. The receptionist was in a place to answer questions and appeared part of the system. The maintenance man drove a university truck and wore a typical university uniform. These are persuasive, especially in an atmosphere where loose procedures and undefined authority seem to hold sway. Here, the first question to be answered is, who should be able to bind the institution to various commitments? Everything, then needs to be detailed and disseminated to all concerned. This would include third parties, such as students and local merchants. Then the rules need to be enforced!

This kind of procedure removes the impact of trappings and apparent authority. It states where real authority lies and communicates this to all concerned. Again, it is not an absolute answer, but it does control the risk involved. A further concern for administrators is that it be totally clear that any contract that is signed, is signed for the institution and not for the individual. When you hire a rock band for a university performance, it is not a contract between you and the band but between the university and the band. You are merely acting as an agent. To avoid personal liability, be sure to add your title to your name. That establishes your "official" capacity and says that you are signing for, and hence binding only, the institution and not yourself as an individual.

DUTIES

In loco parentis is terminally ill, if not dead, but that does not mean that we have no duties to the students who come to our campuses, or to the other guests, tradesmen and even trespassers who travel thereupon. As the section on torts points out, the law imposes a duty that we must meet to keep both ourselves and our institutions free from liability or risk. These are not absolute standards but only reasonable ones. It must be kept in mind that these standards vary as the situation becomes more or less dangerous and the individuals involved more or less capable of dealing with the danger.

Courts do recognize the nature of college students and set a standard of care accordingly. In large measure, the duties involved are common sense duties which reflect the adventuresome spirit of some college students. Dangerous conditions should be corrected and, if they can not be, should be clearly marked and barred to student access. More than that, these conditions need to be identified promptly, and that in turn implies a prompt flow of information. If we were to err here, it should be on the side of conservative action to limit the possibility of risk. Examples of common sense burdens can be found

90

in *Butler* (1976) and *Isaacson* (1975). In *Mintz* (1975), the supreme court in New York held that meeting one's duty was a complete defense.

In all of these cases, the risk referred to is both institutional and personal. In general, the rule of thumb is that acts committed within the scope of employment bind both the individual and the institution. Those committed outside the scope of employment bind only the individual. Of course, some acts within the scope of employment may affect only the individual.

Following the above suggestions may well alleviate many of the possibilities of suit and liability; however, they can not take it to zero. Consequently, some individuals turn to insurance as an answer. It might also be useful to explore the possibility of immunity in public institutions (*Restatement Torts*, 2nd, special note sec. 895B at 21). Keep in mind that, as stated in the chapter in torts, immunity is becoming less and less powerful as a defense.

INSURING AGAINST THE RISK

Before looking at individual policies, check with your institution to see if they have insurance or are self-insured for the purpose of indemnifying personnel who are sued for acts in the scope of employment. Most institutions do offer some form of legal help and indemnification to their employees. For public institutions there is sometimes a state law which provides for legal assistance and indemnification for employees. You should discover how thorough this coverage is before exploring personal insurance. Be sure that it covers the personal liability that could flow from Section 1983 of the Civil Rights Act of 1871 (42 *U.S.C.* 1983). This Act has recently been used by students and employees to challenge the acts and decisions of college administrators (*Wood*, 1975; *Walker*, 1978). The criteria for liability under Section 1983 is that the individual administrator knew or should have known that their actions would result in the deprivation of basic unquestionable constitutional rights. Often, acts leading to liability under Section 1983 may be viewed to be outside the scope of employment and hence not covered by the institution's insurer.

If you have a concern in this area, contact an experienced insurance broker who is familiar with educational problems. Professional associations, such as AAUA, NASPA, and others, may be able to give you information as well. This is an individual decision and one which needs to be met in terms of likelihood of liability and personal desire for coverage.

As stated at the beginning of this chapter, risk is a fact of life and adds both spice and concern. It is not something that should be feared but rather something to be controlled. In general, acting rationally and with good intent can be a successful defense as in *Lister* (1976). Sometimes however, the rules get changed and what had been a protected act becomes ground for liability. In *Tarasoff* (1976), a psychotherapist had depended upon custom and immunity to protect him in a wrongful death action where he had failed to warn the victim. This time it was not sufficient and the doctor was held liable. But in general, common sense will go a long way towards controlling the risk and, hopefully, the comments made above will serve to stimulate that thought process.

REFERENCES

American Law Institute. *Restatement of the law second: Torts 2nd.* St. Paul, Minn.: American Law Institute Publications, 1979.

Table of Cases

Grayned v. City of Rockford, 408 *U.S.* 104 (1972).

Green v. Johns Hopkins Univ., 469 *F. Supp.* 187 (D. Md., 1979).

Gross v. Sweet, 407 *N.Y.S.*2d 254 (S.Ct., App. Div., 3rd Dept., 1978).

Grossner v. Trustees of Columbia University, 287 *F. Supp.* 535 (S.D.N.Y., 1968).

Grove City College v. Bell, 687 *F.*2d 684 (3rd Cir., 1982).

Hall v. Board of Supervisors Southern University, 405 *So.*2d 1125 (La. Ct. App., 1st Cir., 1981).

Hamer v. Sidway, 124 *N.Y.* 538 (1891).

Harrington v. Vandalia-Butler Board of Education, 418 *F. Supp.* 603 (S.D. Oh., 1976).

Healy v. James, 408 *U.S.* 169 (1972).

Heffron v. International Society for Krishna Consciousness, 452 *U.S.* 640 (1981).

Heisler v. New York Medical College, 449 *N.Y.S.*2d 834 (S. Ct, Westchester Cty., 1982).

Hennessy v. Webb, 264 *S.E.*2d 878 (Ga., 1980).

Hoffman v. Red Owl Stores, Inc., 133 *N.W.*2d 267 (Wisc., 1965).

Holzer v. Oakland University Academy of Dramatic Arts, 313 *N.W.*2d 124 (Mich. Ct. App., 1981).

Horton v. Goose Creek Independent School District, 677 *F.*2d 471 (5th Cir., 1982).

In re Tuskegee Institute v. May Refrigeration Co., 344 *So.*2d 156 (Ala., 1977).

Isaacs v. Board of Trustees of Temple University, 385 *F. Supp.* 473 (E.D. Pa.,1974).

Isaacson v. Husson College, 332 *A.*2d 757 (Me., 1975).

Jacobs v. William & Mary, 495 *F. Supp.* 183 (E.D. Va., Newport News Div., 1980).

Jagnandan v. Giles, 538 *F.*2d 1166 (5th Cir., 1976).

James v. Nelson, 349 *F. Supp.* 1061 (N.D. Ill., 1972).

Jesik v. Maricopa City Community College District, 611 *P.*2d 547 (Ariz., 1980).

Jones v. Illinois Department of Rehabilitation Services, 689 *F.*2d 724 (7th Cir., 1982).

Jones v. State Board of Education, 279 *F. Supp.* 190 (M.D. Tenn., 1968).

Jones v. Vassar College, 299 *N.Y.S.*2d 283 (S. Ct. Dutchess Cty., 1969).

Jones v. Wittenberg University, 534 *F.*2d 1203 (6th Cir., 1976).

Joyner v. Whiting, 477 *F.*2d 456 (4th Cir., 1973).

Katz v. United States, 389 *U.S.* 347 (1967).

Keegan v. University of Delaware, 349 *A.*2d 14 (Del., 1975).

Keene v. Rodgers, 316 *F. Supp.* 217 (N.D. Maine, 1970).

Keyishian v. Board of Regents, 385 *U.S.* 589 (1967).

Kline v. Ball, (Pa. Super.), No. J. 1051/82-1 Oct. 1, 1982.

Kline v. 1500 Massachusetts Avenue Corp., 439 *F.*2d 477 (D.C. Cir., 1970).

Koblitz v. Western Reserve University, 21 Ohio Cir. Ct. R. 144 (1901).

Krawez v. Stans, 306 *F. Supp.* 1230 (E.D.N.Y., 1969).

Lefkowitz v. Great Minneapolis Surplus Store, 86 *N.W.*2d 689 (Minn., 1957).

Levine v. George Washington University C.A. 8230-76 (D.C., 1976).

Lindsley v. National Carbonic Gas Company, 220 *U.S.* 61 (1911).

Lister v. Board of Regents of the University of Wisconsin System, 240 *N.W.*2d 610 (Wis., 1976).

Lucy v. Zehmer, 84 *S.E.*2d 516 (Va., 1954).

Marshall v. Barlow's, Inc., 436 *U.S.* 307 (1978).

Marshall v. Maguire, 424 *N.Y.S.*2d 89 (S.Ct. Sp. Term, Nassau Cty., Part 1, 1980).

Marshall v. Marist College, 82 *C.C.H. Lab. Cas.* 33 (S.D.N.Y., 1977).

Marshall v. Regis Educational Corp., No. 80-1835, ____*F.*2d ____ (10th Cir., 1978).

Martinez v. Western Carolina University, 271 *S.E.*2d 91 (N.C. Ct. App., 1980).

Marston v. Gainesville Sun Publishing Company, 341 *So.*2d 783 (Dist. Ct. App. Fla., 1st Dist., 1976).

Mathews v. Eldridge, 424 *U.S.* 319 (1976).

Mazart v. State of New York, 441 *N.Y.S.*2d 600 (Ct. Cl., 1981).

McDonald v. Board of Trustees of the University of Illinois, 375 *F. Supp.* 95 (N.D. Ill., 1974).

McGowan v. Maryland, 366 *U.S.* 420 (1961).

McIntosh v. Milano, 403 *A.*2d 500 (N.J. Super. Ct., Law. Div., 1979).

Meese v. Brigham Young University, 639 *P.*2d 720 (Utah, 1981).

Meyer v. State, 403 *N.Y.S.*2d 420 (Ct. Cl., 1978).

Miller v. California, 413 *U.S.* 15 (1973).

Miller v. Long Island University, 380 *N.Y.S.*2d 917 (S. Ct., Sp. Term, Kings Cty., Part I, 1976).

Mintz v. State, 362 *N.Y.S.*2d 619 (S.Ct., App. Div., 3rd Dept., 1975).

Moore v. Student Affairs Committee of Troy State University, 284 *F. Supp.* 725 (M.D. Ala., 1968).

Morale v. Grigel, 422 *F. Supp.* 988 (D.N.H., 1976).

Nancy P. v. Trustees of Indiana State University, No. 81-7-C (temporary restraining order.) (S.D., Ind., 1981).

National League of Cities v. Usery, 96 *S.Ct.* 2465 (1976).

National Socialist White People's Party v. Ringers, 473 *F.*2d 1010 (4th Cir., 1973).

National Union of Marine Cooks and Stewards v. Arnold, 348 *U.S.* 37 (1954).

New v. Arizona Board of Regents, 618 *P.*2d 238 (Ariz. Ct. App. 1980).

New Times Incorporated v. Arizona Board of Regents, 519 *P.*2d 169 (Ariz., 1974).

North Haven Board of Education v. Bell, 50 *L.W.* 4501 (1982).

North v. Illinois, 27 *N.E.* 54 (Ill., 1891).

Norton v. Discipline Committee of East Tennessee State University, 419 *F.*2d 195 (6th Cir., 1969).

Noto v. United States, 367 *U.S.* 290 (1961).

Nzuve v. Castleton State College, 335 *A.*2d 321 (Vt., 1975).

Papish v. Board of Curators of the University of Missouri, 410 *U.S.* 667 (1973).

Payton v. New York, 445 *U.S.* 573 (1980).

People v. Boettner, 362 *N.Y.S.*2d 365 (S.Ct., Monroe Cty.,1974).

People v. Cohen, 292 *N.Y.S.*2d 706 (Dist. Ct., Nassau Cty., 1st Dist., 1968).

People v. Harfmann, 638 *P.*2d 745 (Colo., 1981).

People v. Lanthier, 97 *Cal. Rptr.* 297 (1971).

People v. Volpe, 452 *N.Y.S.*2d 609 (App. Div., 1982).

People v. Zelinski, 594 *P.*2d 1000 (Cal., 1979).

Peretti v. State of Montana, 464 *F. Supp.* 784 (D. Mont., Missoula Div., 1979).

Perry v. Sindermann, 408 *U.S.* 593 (1972).

Piazzola v. Watkins, 442 *F.*2d 284 (5th Cir., 1971).

Poulin v. Colby College, 402 *A.*2d 846 (Me., 1979).

Poynter v. Drevdahl, 359 *F. Supp.* 1137 (W.D. Mich., N.D. Marquette, 1972).

Prostrollo v. University of South Dakota, 507 *F.*2d 775 (8th Cir., 1974).

R.H. Kyle Furniture Co. v. Russell Dry Goods Co., 340 *S.W.*2d 220 (Ky., 1960).

Racine Unified School District v. Thompson, 321 *N.W.*2d 334 (Wis. App., 1982).

Rakas v. Illinois, 439 *U.S.* 128 (1978).

Reetz v. Michigan, 188 *U.S.* 505 (1903).

Regents of the University of California v. Bakke, 98 *S.Ct.* 2733 (1978).

Relyea v. State, 385 *So.*2d 1378 (Fla. Dist. Ct. App., 1980).

Rendell-Baker v. Kohn, 73 *L.Ed.*2d 418 (1982).

Rice v. Florida Power and Light Co., 363 *So.*2d 834 (Fla. Dist. Ct. App., 1978).

Roberts v. United States, 445 *U.S.* 552 (1980).

Robinson v. The Board of Regents of Eastern Kentucky University, 475 *F.*2d 707 (6th Cir., 1973).

Ronwin v. Shapiro, 657 *F.*2d 1071 (9th Cir., 1981).

Rose v. Nashua Board of Education, 679 *F.*2d 279 (1st Cir., 1982).

Rowan Companies, Inc. v. United States, 49 *L.W.* 4646 (1981).

Ryan v. Hofstra University, 324 *N.Y.S.*2d 964 (S.Ct., Nassau Cty., 1971).

Ryder v. Wescoat, 535 *S.W.*2d 269 (Ct. App. Mo., K.C. Dist., 1976).

St. Ann v. Palisi, 495 *F.*2d 423 (5th Cir., 1974).

Scaduto v. State, 446 *N.Y.S.*2d 529 (App. Div., 1982).

Schiff v. Williams, 519 *F.*2d 257 (5th Cir., 1975).

Schneider v. State, 308 *U.S.* 147 (1939).

Schultz v. Gould Acadamy, 332 *A.*2d 368 (Me., 1975).

Severson v. Elberon Elevator, Inc., 250 *N.W.*2d 417 (Iowa, 1977).

Shamloo v. Mississippi State Board of Trustees, 620 *F.*2d 516 (5th Cir., 1980).

Shannon v. Washington University, 575 *S.W.*2d 235 (Mo. Ct. App., 1978).

Shelton v. Tucker, 364 *U.S.* 479 (1960).

Smith v. Maryland, 442 *U.S.* 735 (1979).

Smyth v. Lubbers, 398 *F. Supp.* 777 (W.D. Mich., 1975).

Sohmer v. Kinnard, 535 *F. Supp.* 50 (D. Md., 1982).

Southeastern Community College v. Davis, 99 *S.Ct.* 2361 (1979).

Southeastern Promotions, Ltd. v. Conrad, 420 *U.S.* 546 (1975).

Spartacus Youth League v. Board of Trustees, 502 *F. Supp.* 789 (N.D. Ill., 1980).

Speake v. Grantham, 317 *F. Supp.* 1253 (S.D. Miss., 1970).

Stanley v. Georgia, 394 *U.S.* 557 (1969).

State ex rel Bartlett v. Pantzer, 489 *P.*2d 375 (Mont., 1971).

State v. Johnson, 530 *P.*2d 910 (Ct. App. Ariz., 1975).

State v. Kappes, 550 *P.*2d 121 (Ariz. App., 1976).

State v. King, 298 *N.W.*2d 168 (Neb., 1980a).

State v. Schmid, 423 *A.*2d 615 (1980). appeal dismissed, 70 *L.Ed.*2d 855 (1982).

State v. Williams, 622 *F.*2d 830 (5th Cir., 1980).

Steier v. New York State Education Commissioner, 271 *F.*2d 13 (2nd Cir., 1959).

Steinberg v. Chicago Medical School, 371 *N.E.*2d 634 (Ill., 1977).

Tarasoff v. Regents of the University of California, 551 *P.*2d 334 (Ca., 1976).

Tedeschi v. Wagner College, 427 *N.Y.S.*2d 760 (1980).

Thonen v. Jenkins, 491 *F.*2d 722 (4th Cir., 1973).

Trujillo v. Love, 322 *F. Supp.* 1266 (D. Colo., 1971).

Turof v. Kibbee, 527 *F. Supp.* 880 (E.D. N.Y., 1981).

United States v. Caceres, 440 *U.S.* 741 (1979a).

United States v. Calandra, 414 *U.S.* 338 (1974).

United States v. Coles, 302 *F. Supp.* 99 (D. Maine, 1969).

United States v. El Camino Community College District, 600 *F.*2d 1258 (9th Cir., 1979).

United States v. Grayson, 438 *U.S.* 41 (1978).

United States v. Havens, 446 *U.S.* 620 (1980a).

United States v. Payner, 447 *U.S.* 727 (1980b).

United States v. Salvucci, 448 *U.S.* 83 (1980).

United States v. Strahan, 674 *F.*2d 96 (1st Cir., 1982).

University of Alaska v. Hendrickson, 552 *P.*2d 148 (Alaska, 1976).

University of Richmond v. Bell, 543 *F. Supp.* 321 (E.D. Va. Richmond Div., 1982).

University Realty and Development Co. v. Omid-Gaf, Inc., 508 *P.*2d 747 (Ct. App. Az., Div. 2, 1973).

Uzzell v. Friday, 591 *F.*2d 997 (4th Cir., 1979).

Villalobos v. University of Oregon, 614 *P.*2d 107 (Or. Ct. App., 1980).

Walter v. United States, 447 *U.S.* 649 (1980).

Walker v. University of Pittsburgh, 457 *F. Supp.* 1000 (W.D. Pa., 1978).

Washington v. Chrisman, 102 *S.Ct.* 812 (1982).

Whiteside v. Kay, 446 *F. Supp.* 716 (W.D. La., 1978).

Widmar v. Vincent, 70 *L.Ed.*2d 440 (1981).

Wisconsin v. Constantineau, 400 *U.S.* 433 (1971).

Wood v. Strickland, 420 *U.S.* 308 (1975).

Woods v. Simpson, 146 Md. 547 (1924).

Wright v. Columbia University, 520 *F. Supp.* 789 (E.D. Pa., 1981).

Wright v. Texas Southern University, 392 *F.*2d. 728 (5th Cir., 1968).

Zanders v. Louisiana State Board of Education, 281 *F. Supp.* 747 (W.D. La., 1968).

Zavala v. Regents of the University of California, 178 *Cal. Rptr.* 185 (Ct. App., 1981).

Appendix A

United States Courts of Appeals

Circuit	Geographic Area Covered
First	Rhode Island, Massachusetts, New Hampshire, Maine, Puerto Rico
Second	Vermont, Connecticut, New York
Third	Pennsylvania, New Jersey, Delaware, Virgin Islands
Fourth	Maryland, Virginia, West Virginia, North Carolina, South Carolina
Fifth	Mississippi, Louisiana, Texas, Canal Zone
Sixth	Ohio, Michigan, Kentucky, Tennessee
Seventh	Indiana, Illinois, Wisconsin
Eighth	Minnesota, North Dakota, South Dakota, Iowa, Nebraska, Missouri, Arkansas
Ninth	California, Oregon, Nevada, Washington, Idaho, Montana, Hawaii, Alaska, Arizona, Guam
Tenth	Colorado, Wyoming, Utah, Kansas, Oklahoma, New Mexico
Eleventh*	Alabama, Florida, Georgia
The District of Columbia	Separate Judicial Circuit

*Prior to October 14, 1982, Alabama, Florida, and Georgia were part of the 5th Circuit. (PL96-452, 10/14/80).

Appendix B

National Reporter System

There is a national reporter system which provides for the reporting of court decisions by means of the publications listed below. In some cases one or more publications will cover the decisions of a single court, as with the U.S. Supreme Court. In other cases a single publication may contain court decisions in a geographical area, as is the case with Regional Reporters

Abbreviation   Publication

The United States Supreme Court
U.S.   *United States Reports.*

S.Ct.   *Supreme Court Reports.*

L.Ed.2d   *Lawyers Edition,* Second Series.

L.W.   *United States Law Week.* From time to time a Supreme Court decision will be reported in *Law Week* before it is published in the other reporters.

F.R.D.   *Federal Rules Decisions.* Reports decisions of United States district courts not reported in the *Federal Supplement.*

The United States Courts of Appeals
F.2d   *The Federal Reporter,* Second Series.

The United States District Courts
F. Supp.   *The Federal Supplement.*

State Courts, Reported in Regional Reporters
N.E.2d   *Northeastern Reporter,* Second Series. Massachusetts, Rhode Island, New York, Ohio, Indiana, and Illinois.

A.2d	*Atlantic Reporter*, Second Series. Maine, New Hampshire, Vermont, Connecticut, New Jersey, Pennsylvania, Delaware, and Maryland.
So.2d	*Southern Reporter*, Second Series. Florida, Alabama, Mississippi, and Louisiana.
S.E.2d	*Southeastern Reporter*, Second Series. Virginia, West Virginia, North Carolina, South Carolina, and Georgia.
S.W.2d	*Southwestern Reporter*, Second Series. Kentucky, Tennessee, Missouri, Arkansas, and Texas.
P.2d	*Pacific Reporter*, Second Series. Alaska, Hawaii, Montana, Wyoming, Idaho, Kansas, Colorado, Oklahoma, New Mexico, Utah, Arizona, Nevada, Washington, Oregon, and California.
N.W.2d	*Northwestern Reporter*, Second Series. Michigan, Wisconsin, Iowa, Minnesota, North Dakota, South Dakota, and Nebraska.
N.Y.S.2d	*New York Supplement*, Second Series. Certain New York state courts. Some of these cases may also be reported in *N.E.*2d.
Cal.Rptr.	*California Reporter*. California. Some of these cases will also appear in *P.*2d. The *Cal. Rptr.* was started in 1960 and California cases decided prior to 1969 can be found in *P.*2d.

Appendix C

Federal Laws Affecting
College and University Housing

Age Discrimination in Employment Act of 1967
29 *U.S.C.* 621 with Interpretations at 29 *C.F.R.* 860.

Age Discrimination Act of 1975
42 *U.S.C.* 6101.

Copyright Revision Act
Title 17 United States Code with regulations at 37 *C.F.R.* 201, 202, 203, 204.

Equal Pay Act of 1963
29 *U.S.C.* 206(d) with regulations at 29 *C.F.R.* 806.

Executive Order 11246 as amended
32 *F.R.* 14303 with regulations at 41 *C.F.R.* 60 and 41 *C.F.R.* 60-2. Employee Selection Guidelines Appear at 41 *F.R.* 29016.

Fair Labor Standards Act of 1938
29 *U.S.C.* 201.

Family Educational Rights and Privacy Act (Buckley Amendment)
20 *U.S.C.* 1232(g) with regulations at 34 *C.F.R.* 99.

Human Subjects Research
45 *C.F.R.* 46.

Occupational Safety and Health Act of 1970 (OSHA)
29 *U.S.C.* 651 with regulations at 29 *C.F.R.* 42, 29 *C.F.R.* 1903 and 41 *C.F.R.* 29-70.

Privacy Act of 1974
5 *U.S.C.* 552a. Each agency issues regulations.
The Department of Education regulations appear at 34 *C.F.R.* 5.

Rehabilitation Act of 1973 (Section 504)
29 *U.S.C.* 794 with regulations at 34 *C.F.R.* 104.

Title VI (Civil Rights Act of 1964)
42 *U.S.C.* 2000(d) with regulations at 34 *C.F.R.* 100.

Title VII (Civil Rights Act of 1964)
42 *U.S.C.* 2000 (e)2 with regulations at 29 *C.F.R.* 1601 and sexual harassment guidelines at 24 *C.F.R.* 1604.

Title IX (Education Amendments of 1972)
20 *U.S.C.* 1681 and regulations at 34 *C.F.R.* 100.

Appendix D

Checklist of
Housing Legal Issues

This list of questions is intended as an aid in auditing your housing programs, policies and practices. The list may also be used as a tool in a staff development program. Questions are arranged by the chapter to which they refer. Thus, if you are unclear about your response to a particular question, you may want to read that chapter again to be sure you understand the parameters involved. The questions are not intended to be an exhaustive list but only a representative sample of common concerns.

Chapter II
Constitutional Issues in the Residence Halls

1. Have you developed a written policy pertaining to freedom of expression in the residence halls? Will commercial solicitation be prohibited? What restrictions, if any, will you place on political canvassing?
2. If you are responsible for a student publication, have you advised the editors about the law of libel and the legal definition of "obscenity"?
3. What are your policies pertaining to recognition of student groups and the use of campus facilities by those groups? Do you restrict or deny recognition to student groups on the basis of social, political, or religious views which they espouse?
4. Do you have a written policy pertaining to searches of student rooms? Have your employees been informed about the privacy rights of students?
5. Have you established guidelines for cooperation with law enforcement authorities when student rooms are to be searched for illegal drugs, or in other cases which might result in criminal prosecution?

6. Have you made a reasonable effort to inform students in advance, of the general forms of prohibited behavior on your campus?

7. Have you established a simple, informal procedure to resolve minor disciplinary cases? If you believe your rules are too "legalistic," have you consulted with a lawyer about the "due process" standards which the courts have required at colleges and universities? Do you simply follow the "criminal court" model without considering the dangers of proceduralism in an educational setting?

8. If you believe you need a psychiatric withdrawal policy, have you developed a policy which sets clear and unambiguous standards for withdrawal? Is your policy so vague that it can be misused to remove students who are merely eccentric or unpopular, or who express controversial political views? Have you established a due process procedure for psychiatric withdrawals?

9. Have you considered other alternatives to "group billing" or punishment? Do you have a procedure which allows students to establish that they did not participate in any misbehavior by a group of students? Do you impose only minor penalties in such cases?

Chapter III
Statutes and Regulations Affecting Residence Hall Operations and Staff

1. Do you know the law of your state pertaining to consumption or furnishing of (a) beer, (b) wine, (c) liquor? Does your state have a Dramshop law? Does your state recognize a social host liability? Is this information used to educate residents concerning their responsibilities and possible liabilities?

2. Are all of your educational programs accessible to the handicapped? Have you read your institutional self-study regarding Section 504?

3. Are your residential facilities, policies, practices, and fees comparable for men and women? What steps have you taken to assure that off-campus listings are comparable in quality and cost for both men and women? Have you read or reviewed your institutional self-study regarding Title IX?

4. Is there a quota of residential spaces set aside for any ethnic group(s) on campus?

5. Are your staff trained with respect to (1) the types of questions which may and may not be asked during interviews of prospective employees, (2) procedures to follow to report violations of antidiscrimination laws? Do you follow the Affirmative Action plan of your institution when you employ staff?

6. Do you have a grievance procedure established to handle complaints concerning discrimination and sexual harassment? Does your procedure accommodate both students and staff?

7. Has the housing staff been included in the definition of "school officials" in your institutional Buckley Policy? Has the staff been trained to know what information may and may not be disclosed without a student's consent?

Chapter IV
Contracts and Their Use in Housing

1. Do you have a written housing agreement? Does it reflect your actual procedures?

2. What are other university offices saying about Housing? Do admissions, athletics, alumni, etc., make representations that accurately reflect *your* policies?

3. Are your housing assignment details specific? Do the students know them? Are they adhered to?

4. Do you normally review your rules and regulations in advance of any contract signing? Are all pertinent rules and regulations up-to- date and available to students at the time of contract signing?

5. Are both your professional and non-professional staffs aware of their roles and the possibility of their binding the university?

6. Does your offer of housing clearly specify what is being offered and how an acceptance is to be made? Do you permit alternative means of acceptance? Should you?

7. Have you developed specific and detailed procedures for early termination? What, if any, refund will you make? How will you confirm dietary, medical, psychological, or religious problems?

Chapter V
Torts: Your Legal Duties and Responsibilities

1. Do you provide regular training sessions for staff and employees, with an emphasis on increasing their awareness of possible liability-imposing situations? Are they aware that their actions or inactions may result in liability against them and/or the university?

2. Do you have standardized procedures which provide for the routine inspection and repair of residence hall facilities by maintenance, custodial or other staff employees?

3. Do you have standardized procedures regarding the supervision of on-campus and off-campus residence hall activities sponsored by the Housing Department?

4. Do you maintain standardized procedures and provide regular staff training for handling emergencies such as fires, injuries, equipment failure, etc.?
5. Do you have a policy for coping with the risks associated with the loss of a residence hall master key by an employee?
6. Do you employ and rely upon "release forms" in an attempt to avoid tort liability?
7. Do you communicate regularly with the university counsel or the risk management department?

Chapter VI
Managing the Risk

1. Do your rules and regulations reflect your actual procedures? Which don't? What actions are you taking with respect to those that do not?
2. Are your purchasing procedures set for procurement? Do all of your employees know them? Do third party merchants/suppliers know them?
3. Do you have formal procedures for handling student complaints? Do the students know them? Do you follow them?
4. Are you kept up to date on hazardous conditions in the residence halls? Do you respond promptly to conditions as they arise?
5. Are you aware of activities or trends that the students are now engaging in? Do they present you with a duty or possible liability?
6. Is there an implied warranty of habitability in your state? Does it apply to university housing?
7. Does your state law in any way shield you from suit? Under what conditions?